Merry Christmas
2

MW00608872

Love,
Caroline

TASTING
KENTUCKY
Favorite Recipes from the Bluegrass State

by Maggie Green

photography by Sarah Jane Sanders
foreword by Ouita Michel

FARCOUNTRY
PRESS

For Kentucky cooks and bakers
who stand in a kitchen every day to put
a wholesome meal on the table.

ISBN: 978–1–56037–653–8

© 2016 by Farcountry Press
Text © 2016 by Maggie Green
Photography © 2016 by Sarah Jane Sanders
Back cover: Pinnacles near Berea, photo by Alexey Stiop, Thinkstock by Getty Images
Pages ii and iii: Manchester Horse Farm, photo by Alexey Stiop, Thinkstock by Getty Images
Page iv: Cumberland Falls, photo by Linda Doane; www.DoanePhoto.com

For more information on our books, write Farcountry Press,
P.O. Box 5630, Helena, MT 59604; call (800) 821–3874; or visit
www.farcountrypress.com.

Library of Congress Cataloging–in–Publication Data on file.

Produced in the United States of America. Printed in China.

20   19   18   17   16   1   2   3   4   5

contents

chapter 1: Breakfast & Brunch

chapter 2: Appetizers & Snacks

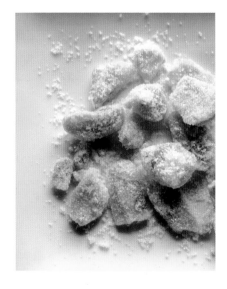

chapter 3: Salads & Sides

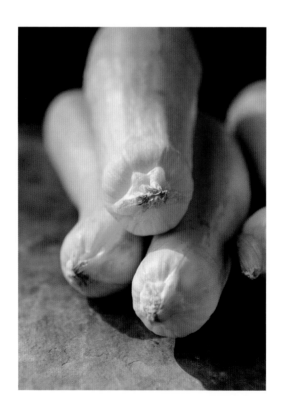

chapter 4: Soups & Stews

chapter 5: Main Courses

chapter 6: Desserts & Sweet Treats

acknowledgments

by Maggie Green

Just like any other book, a cookbook involves many moving parts and isn't written alone or in a vacuum. In thanks for their role in its completion, I'd like to recognize those who contributed to this cookbook.

Thanks to my editor Will Harmon, designer Shirley Machonis, and all the professionals at Farcountry Press who took my manuscript and turned it into a finished book.

Hugs, and good lighting always, to photographer—and now, I'm happy to say, friend—Sarah Jane Sanders. We spent hours together in my kitchen, and behind her camera, to bring these recipes to life. We weathered snow and thunderstorms, chased light around my house, and worked to take photographs of every recipe in this book. I am now a better cookbook author for having worked with smart, talented, and professional Sarah Jane.

Please give a round of applause to the more than fifty chefs who contributed their recipes for use in this cookbook. They eagerly shared recipes, cooking techniques, and not least their passion for great food.

Special thanks to Ouita Michel. A friend from the "old days" of Girl Scouts when we grew up together in Lexington, she is generous and a great promoter of Kentucky food. She cares about people, she cares about cooking, and she cares about Kentucky. Thank you for writing the foreword to this book and for your recipes from your restaurants. Kentucky is lucky to have someone like Ouita on the front lines of local food and drink, promoting food, ingredients, farmers, jobs, and traditions.

Next, an appreciative shout-out to my friend Sara Gibbs. Sara and I trained together in Culinary Arts at the National Center for Hospitality Studies many years ago. Sara remains immersed in food, cooking, and farming, while I remain immersed in cookbooks, cooking, and raising a family. Despite the different paths our lives followed, I know that she's just a text message or e-mail away when a food or recipe question pops up or I want to say hi and check in. Generous, helpful, and kind, Sara assisted in obtaining several recipes in this book and provided recommendations on others to contact as well.

Special thanks to my mother for laying a foundation in my life that included the importance of feeding people home-prepared food. Your silver julep cups and a few pieces of pottery came in handy on this project. Thanks too, to you and Dad, for showing me the good things about Kentucky food, traditions, trips, and people.

Fist bump to my seven siblings: Kaye for her photography advice and help in the test kitchen, Theresa for texting and e-mailing tips about photography and content, Anne for connections at Shaker Village and with our friend Ouita, Barbara for offering use of her Frankfort kitchen with its beautiful surfaces and lighting, Mary for keeping her book club well fed with food from my first cookbook (and now I hope this book will keep them well fed, too), Frances for nudges to move forward with this cookbook, and Carl for reminding me that it's not breakfast without a fresh doughnut, omelet, or pancake. You guys are the best. I don't know of any cookbook author who has such a talented, built-in group of advisors who are only a text message, phone call, or car ride away. Thanks too, to their spouses Kevin, Jack, Mike, Stewart, Bob, Bill, and Dawn and Warren's family Nina, Wayne, Tara, Lori, Sam, Michael, and Ana. You guys are my family too, and for that I am happy.

To Stuart, Julia, and Neil: you've been a part of another cookbook and I'm so glad you were. I'm a better cook because of you all, a better recipe tester because of your honesty, and a better mother because we've shared our home, kitchen, and table with each other. As you leave our nest, the greatest gift you can give to others is to share what you have learned about food and cooking with people you care about. You'll soon understand that the ability to cook and discern good food is not only a gift for them, but a gift to yourself as well.

And finally to Warren: you're last on this list, but not least. In fact, it's your unwavering commitment to our family that kept things ticking along when Sarah Jane was due to come over or when I was up against a deadline. If someone wants to learn how to be a supportive spouse, they only need look to you to see that you're not in this just for the food, but also for the good of those you care about.

And to all my fellow citizens of Kentucky who take the time to grow, share, and cook for family and friends, I thank you. If it wasn't for what we do in our homes every day and for the shared commitment to use what's bountiful and plentiful in our beautiful Bluegrass State, this book wouldn't exist. The sun does shine bright on our old Kentucky homes.

foreword

by Ouita Michel

Kentucky's family farms, 85,000 strong, have deeply influenced the course of its history, economy, and food culture. One of Kentucky's leading exports, our delicious bourbon, is firmly rooted in Kentucky's corn production. For more than 200 years, we have distilled corn into this elixir, and still today Kentucky is among the top corn-producing states in the nation. It is evident also in what we eat: cornbread, corn cakes, grits, spoon bread, corn pudding—all traditional Kentucky favorites.

Kentucky boasts a livestock industry second to none, raising beef, hogs, chickens, lamb, goat, rabbit, and even squab (pigeon). Increasingly this livestock is processed here instead of being shipped to other states, and more and more Kentuckians are enjoying the delicious flavors of grass-finished beef, pork, and local chicken.

Chefs and cooks from across the Commonwealth are involved in celebrating and preparing Kentucky-produced foodstuffs through a Department of Agriculture program called Kentucky Proud, which helps brand locally produced products for consumers. Together we have boiled up local freshwater prawns; sliced up Kentucky-made cheese boards; picked blueberries, strawberries, apples, plums, and pears at local orchards; even slathered delicious Kentucky caviar on corn cakes. We have made tomato pies and pickled peppers, fried up breakfast sausage, whipped up eggs, and even picked pawpaws and persimmons grown here in Kentucky.

The diversity of our farming community has deeply inspired me as a chef. The beauty of this farm-fresh food is always breathtaking: multiple varieties of Swiss chard, mustard greens, lettuces, herbs, beans, tomatoes, eggplant, squash . . . the list is endless. One farmer I know grew twenty-six varieties of potato! This diversity brings me so much joy in my cooking and leaves me grateful to live and work in such a beautiful place.

Maggie Green has compiled recipes from every region of Kentucky, representing chefs, cooks, and farmers themselves. These recipes reflect our ever-changing food culture. Sarah Jane Sanders's photographs bring the recipes to life. It thrills me to know that the bounty I have enjoyed as a Kentucky chef will make its way into kitchens across America.

introduction

Except for a three-year stint after college, I've always lived in Kentucky. Kentucky is not just a place where I lay my head at night, but it's also my home. Every part of the Bluegrass State—from northern Kentucky where I now live and have raised my three children; to central Kentucky where I grew up and went to grade school, high school, and college; to western Kentucky where I've explored caves, lakes, and towns; to eastern Kentucky where I've worked in hospitals and made home health visits— it all draws me in. I've seen the mountain grandeur and the green, green grass of horse farms. From root to tip, from stem to stern, among the people and on the land, Kentucky is where I belong.

In my family, all my children, both of my parents, and all four of my grandparents eventually called Kentucky home. Kentucky offered something that they maybe could have found elsewhere, but that they chose to find here. Some were born here, but in the end they all lived and worked here. Drove buses and went to church here. Built roads and bridges here. Raised their families here and took advantage of the historic sites, state parks, horse farms, countryside, and sense of place that Kentucky offers.

Anyone who spends any time in Kentucky will tell you that you can't travel and enjoy the scenery or visit family or friends without a bite to eat. No matter where you go or what you do in the Bluegrass State, it's not a gathering unless you share some food and drink.

At a Kentucky foodways event sponsored by the University of Kentucky Special Collections Library, panel moderator John van Willigen reminisced about one of the first meals he was served when he visited Kentucky. One Sunday afternoon in a friend's south-central Kentucky home, van Willigen had the opportunity to stay for dinner. He described on the table a platter of fried chicken that was hot and golden-brown. But it wasn't this platter of chicken that impressed him. It was the side dishes that surrounded the platter of chicken—much of it from the garden that grew just outside the back door or from the jars of food preserved from last year's garden bounty—that made the meal. Sliced red tomatoes, green beans cooked with ham, steamy corn pudding, flaky biscuits, and

thick-sliced sweet pickles, all piled high in bowls and strewn across the table, as the supporting cast for the chicken.

When I look back, that's pretty much the way most meals that I remember were served, too. Our large family ate dinner together almost every night of every week. My mom cooked meatloaf, roast beef, or pork roast and then on the side served the fresh stuff—sliced red or fried green tomatoes, sometimes tomato aspic, green beans, corn on the cob, mashed potatoes, bread dumplings, corn pudding, pickled beets, red cabbage, baked beans, watermelon balls, or cooked apples.

Outside of Kentucky homes, meals in family- or chef-owned Kentucky restaurants, cafés, B&Bs, and inns are prepared in much the same way, offering what's fresh, abundant, and available, sometimes from a garden out the back door or a nearby farmer or food producer. Drive across the state from east to west and from north to south, and you'll find regional variations in Kentucky foods—from Appalachia to central Kentucky's horse farms, and from the German-influenced cities in northern Kentucky to the barbecue of the west. But the underlying current is the same: how can we make the most of what we have and put a fresh, wholesome meal on the table. Ingredients typically include beef, pork, wild game, black walnuts, wild pecans, hickory, mutton, corn, spring water, distilled spir-its, beans, tomatoes, and a whole host of other fresh vegetables. Cooking methods that preserve food for later: smoking, pickling, fermenting, canning, and curing all show up when you eat a meal in Kentucky. Whether at someone's home or at the table of a chef who understands Kentucky's food and its connection to the land, you're going to eat some of the most delicious food found anywhere in the country.

With four other state-inspired cookbooks under their belt, Farcountry Press embarked on a journey east of the Mississippi River. Lucky for me, and lucky for you, they landed in Kentucky. It's no accident, at least as far as I can see, that Kentucky was the first state they chose for a cook-book from the eastern corridor of the United States.

Kentucky was a land of promise for immigrants and settlers who explored and made their way through the Cumberland Gap from Virginia

or through Ellis Island to Kentucky. Immigrants from Germany, Ireland, and Scotland and settlers from the English colonies to the east were offered and saw promise in land that was new, fresh, and abundant. They brought with them their traditions of agriculture, smoking, distilling, and farming. These all influenced the food we find today in Kentucky. The state's culinary traditions are unique, a subset of Southern cuisine unmatched in any other southern state. We've got it all here in Kentucky —diverse people, diverse traditions, diverse heritage; world-class sporting events and top-notch college sports; lakes, rivers, farmland, and mountains—all intersecting to provide ingredients, cooking techniques, and grand occasions that bring everyone to a table spread with food and traditions that only Kentucky can offer.

As the Kentucky-based food writer selected to write this cookbook, my job was to collect 100 recipes from chefs and restaurants across the state that best express Kentucky food—the flavors, tastes, and ingredients that make Kentucky unique. The first thing one does here in Kentucky when embarking on such a project is to "ask around." Suggestions flooded in, and I connected with some of the most talented chefs and cooks in the Kentucky hospitality industry. The hard part, for me, was that had I been given more time, I probably could have found 200 recipes to feature instead of 100, from at least fifty more restaurants. But with every project, there's a deadline, and an end to the gathering stage.

So what I present and share is the spirit of Kentucky cuisines as expressed through the creations of chefs and cooks in restaurants, inns, cafés, farms, and food trucks across the state. Recipes from these chefs and establishments will allow home cooks to re-create a sampling of iconic and contemporary Kentucky recipes using fresh, abundant ingredients. Some ingredients might be available out your back door, some from the supermarket, and some specialty ingredients might only be available by ordering from a Kentucky food producer or farmer; nonetheless these ingredients will add a Kentucky flair to your cooking. Enjoy!

—Maggie Green

guidelines for recipes

❧ Temperatures are listed in degrees Fahrenheit.

❧ Fresh produce should be washed before using.

❧ Garlic, onions, carrots, and potatoes should be peeled before use unless otherwise noted.

❧ All-purpose flour was used in testing any recipe calling for flour. If a recipe needed different flour, either cake or pastry flour is listed.

❧ Sugar refers to white granulated sugar unless otherwise noted.

❧ Butter is unsalted butter unless otherwise noted.

❧ Salt is iodized table salt unless otherwise noted in the recipes where coarse or kosher salt is important or directed by the chef or restaurant.

❧ Pepper refers to freshly ground black pepper.

❧ Eggs used in testing were large eggs.

❧ Bread crumbs vary in this book: dry, fresh, or panko. For best results, use the type called for in the recipe.

❧ Nuts may be toasted in a small pan on the stove. Spread the nuts in a skillet and cook over medium heat, stirring, until nuts begin to brown and become aromatic. They can burn quickly, so watch them carefully and pour into a bowl when done.

Breakfast & Brunch

Lemon Soufflé Pancakes with Blueberry Compote, p. 12

Bacon-Cheddar Scones

SPOONFUL OF SUGAR . . . SWEETS AND SUCH, MOUNT STERLING
CHEF STEPHEN POWELL

Spoonful of Sugar bakes homemade pastries such as these savory scones, made with Broadbent bacon, every day. These are best eaten still warm from the oven or within one day of baking.

Preheat the oven to 425 degrees. Line a baking sheet with parchment paper.

In a skillet, fry the bacon. Drain, cool, and then crumble into small pieces.

In a bowl, whisk together the flour, salt, sugar, and baking powder. With a pastry cutter, work in the butter until crumbly. Add the shredded cheese, green onions, and bacon. Stir in the 1 cup of heavy cream until combined.

Turn the dough onto a lightly floured surface. Roll or pat the dough into a 7-inch disk. Cut into eight wedges and place on the prepared baking sheet.

Lightly brush the top of each scone with heavy whipping cream. Bake until golden brown, 20 to 22 minutes.

⅓ pound bacon (about 6 slices)

2 cups flour

½ teaspoon salt

2 teaspoons sugar

1 tablespoon baking powder

4 tablespoons (½ stick) butter,
    cut into slices

1 cup shredded Cheddar cheese

½ cup finely diced green onions

1 cup heavy cream,
    plus 2 tablespoons
    for brushing on scones

Makes 8 scones

4 russet baking potatoes

¼ cup vegetable oil

1 teaspoon salt

½ teaspoon black pepper

Serves 4

Breakfast Potatoes

AURORA LANDING RESTAURANT, HARDIN
KENLAKE STATE RESORT PARK
DIRECTOR OF FOOD SERVICES THOMAS BROWN

Aurora Landing overlooks Kentucky Lake at Kenlake State Resort Park. Kentucky boasts the largest developed state park system in the country with seventeen resort parks that have full-service lodges and restaurants. The state park system's restaurants support the Kentucky Proud agricultural marketing program and use locally grown meats and produce when available. These breakfast potatoes with a scrumptious crust are a simple addition to eggs, sausage, or any main breakfast entrée.

Wash the potatoes, skins on, and place them in a big pot. Add water to cover the potatoes. Bring to a boil, reduce heat to a simmer, and cook until the potatoes are easily pierced with a fork, about 25 minutes. Drain and let cool, then peel and cut into ⅜-inch-thick slices.

Heat the oil on a griddle or in a large skillet over medium-high heat. Add the potatoes, sprinkle with salt and pepper, and cook until brown on one side and a crust forms, about 10 minutes. Turn and brown on the other side, about 10 more minutes. Serve with ketchup or hot sauce.

Bourbon-vanilla whipped butter

½ cup (1 stick) butter, softened

½ cup powdered sugar

2 tablespoons Kentucky bourbon

1 teaspoon vanilla extract

Pancakes

3 cups flour

3 tablespoons sugar

1 tablespoon baking powder

1 tablespoon baking soda

Pinch salt

3 eggs

3 cups buttermilk

2 tablespoons vanilla extract

1 tablespoon butter or vegetable oil

Maple syrup

Makes 12 large pancakes

Buttermilk Pancakes with Bourbon-Vanilla Whipped Butter

RED RIVER ROCKHOUSE, CAMPTON
AARON AND TINA BROUWER

This café tucked into the Red River Gorge serves wholesome meals made from produce grown by local farmers and ranchers. Weisenberger Mill's all-purpose flour is a favorite at the Rockhouse for making these griddle cakes.

For the bourbon-vanilla whipped butter:
With an electric mixer, beat the butter until soft and fluffy, about 2 minutes. Mix in the powdered sugar, bourbon, and vanilla.

For the pancakes:
In a large bowl, whisk together the flour, sugar, baking powder, baking soda, and salt.

In a separate bowl, whisk the eggs. Add the buttermilk and vanilla, and whisk vigorously until combined.

Pour the wet mixture into the dry mixture and fold together using a rubber spatula. Combine until it's mixed, but not over-mixed.

Preheat a griddle or frying pan over medium-high heat. Grease the griddle with the butter or oil. Flick water across the surface—if it beads up and sizzles, it's ready. Pour or scoop the batter onto the griddle, using ½ cup for each pancake. Brown on both sides. Serve with the bourbon-vanilla whipped butter and warm maple syrup.

4 large, firm, tart apples
such as Gala

3 tablespoons butter

¼ cup granulated sugar

¼ teaspoon cinnamon

Pinch salt

¼ cup brown sugar

1 teaspoon apple cider vinegar

Serves 4

Fried Apples

HOLLY HILL INN, MIDWAY   ❧   CHEF OUITA MICHEL

A perfect side dish for breakfast or with a pork chop dinner. Reed Valley Orchard supplies Chef Ouita with the perfect apples for this dish, and she'll use whichever variety they recommend.

Wash but do not peel the apples. Core and slice into thin wedges.

Melt the butter in a large skillet over medium-high heat. Add the apples, granulated sugar, cinnamon, and salt. Cook for 5 minutes, turning occasionally.

Lower heat and cook, uncovered, until almost all liquid has evaporated, about 5 more minutes.

Sprinkle with brown sugar and vinegar and continue to cook until some of the apples have caramelized along the edge, about 15 minutes. Serve hot or at room temperature.

Goetta (Hog n' Oats Sausage)

FORK IN THE ROAD MOBILE GALLEY, LEXINGTON
CHEF MARK JENSEN

This rustic breakfast meat features a savory blend of ground pork, ground beef, and two types of oats. A loaf pan makes the perfect mold for shaping the mixture. After chilling, cut it into thick slices, pan-fry, and serve.

6 cups (1½ quarts) beef stock

1½ tablespoons salt

1 tablespoon black pepper

2 cups pinhead or steel-cut oats

1 cup rolled oats

3 bay leaves

3 garlic cloves

3 allspice berries,
    or ¼ teaspoon ground allspice

1 teaspoon fresh thyme leaves,
    or ½ teaspoon dried thyme

1 pound ground pork shoulder

1 pound ground beef chuck

Vegetable oil

Each loaf serves 8 to 10

In a deep, heavy-bottomed pot, bring the stock to a simmer.

Add the salt, black pepper, both oats, and bay leaves. Crush and add the garlic (a microplane works well to make a garlic paste). Grind and add the allspice if using whole berries, or add the ground allspice. Add the thyme leaves. Keep the stock, oats, and spices at a low simmer for 60 minutes. Stir often, minding the bottom to keep a crust from forming.

Add the pork and beef to the oats and stock. Stir well to combine. Cover and cook at a low simmer for an additional 2 hours. Continue to stir often, again to avoid a crust forming.

Meanwhile, grease two 9 x 5-inch loaf pans with nonstick spray.

After 2 hours, remove the sausage mixture from the heat; it's fully cooked at this point. Remove the bay leaves. Taste to check the seasoning; add more salt and pepper if desired.

Divide the mixture between the two prepared loaf pans. Press down to smooth the top and compact the mixture. Wrap tightly with plastic wrap. Refrigerate overnight to set the sausage.

To prepare:
Unwrap the goetta and turn it out of the loaf pan. Slice into thick slices. Heat the oil over medium-high heat in a skillet or on a griddle. Cook each slice of goetta until both sides are browned, crispy, and sizzling. Serve with fried eggs and hash browns, as a side to pancakes, or with curried lentils (*see recipe in the Main Courses section, page 100*).

¼ cup warm water

1 package (2¼ teaspoons)
    active-dry yeast

¼ cup plus 1 teaspoon sugar,
    divided

7 cups self-rising flour

1½ teaspoons salt

1½ tablespoons baking powder

1 cup (2 sticks) butter,
    cut into slices

2½ cups buttermilk

4 tablespoons (½ stick) butter,
    melted

Makes 12 large biscuits

Gold Rush Yeast Biscuits

GOLD RUSH CAFE   OWNER KENNETH WHITE

Biscuits at Gold Rush are large and fluffy. Much like a popular southern biscuit called Angel Biscuits, these biscuits contain yeast and baking powder, which ensures a tender interior.

In a bowl, mix together the water, yeast, and 1 teaspoon sugar. Set aside.

In a separate bowl, combine the remaining ¼ cup of sugar with the flour, salt, and baking powder. Add the butter and use two knives or a pastry cutter to cut in the butter to the size of small peas. Stir in the yeast mixture and buttermilk. Mix until well combined and a very soft dough forms. Cover with plastic wrap or a damp towel and let rise in a warm spot of the kitchen until double in size, about 1 hour.

Grease two baking sheets.

Remove half of the dough and place it on a lightly floured surface. Sprinkle the top of the dough lightly with flour. Being careful not to overwork the dough or add too much flour, roll to about ½ inch thick. Use a 3-inch round cutter to cut out the biscuits. Place the biscuits on the baking sheet, leaving a little gap between each biscuit. Repeat with the remaining dough, adding the trimmings back each time. Brush the uncooked biscuits with melted butter. Let rise in a warm place for 30 minutes.

Preheat the oven to 400 degrees.

Bake until lightly browned, 22 to 25 minutes. Serve immediately.

Cream gravy

1 tablespoon bacon grease

1 tablespoon flour

¼ teaspoon salt

⅛ teaspoon black pepper

1 cup milk

Cornmeal biscuits

1¾ cups flour

¼ cup stone-ground cornmeal

2 teaspoons baking powder

¼ teaspoon baking soda

½ teaspoon salt

6 tablespoons (¾ stick)
    cold butter

¾ cup buttermilk

Kentucky Eggs Benedict

ISLAND VIEW RESTAURANT, BURKESVILLE
DALE HOLLOW LAKE STATE RESORT PARK
DIRECTOR OF FOOD SERVICES THOMAS BROWN

At Kentucky state parks, travelers can enjoy a variety of menu selections from traditional Kentucky cuisine. To add to the atmosphere, this restaurant has three walls of glass that allow you to embrace the breathtaking view of Dale Hollow Lake and its islands. This twist on classic eggs Benedict is made with cornmeal biscuits.

For the cream gravy:
Heat the bacon grease over medium heat until melted. Add the flour and continue to cook until lightly browned, about 2 minutes. Add the salt and pepper. Stir in the milk and whisk until thick and the flour taste is cooked out, about 5 minutes. Add black pepper or salt to taste.

For the cornmeal biscuits:
Preheat the oven to 450 degrees. Have ready one ungreased 11 x 7 x 1-inch baking pan.

Whisk together the flour, cornmeal, baking powder, baking soda, and salt. With a box grater, grate the cold butter into the flour using the large holes on the grater. With your hands, gently mix the butter and flour to coat the butter in flour and break up any large butter particles. Stir in the buttermilk just to combine. Avoid over-stirring or the biscuits may be tough.

Turn the dough onto a lightly floured surface and knead about four times to form a soft dough. Pat or roll until about ½-inch thick. Cut the dough into rounds with a biscuit cutter or small juice glass dipped in flour. Place on the pan with the edges touching. Bake until the biscuits are golden brown, 15 to 18 minutes.

Eggs Benedict

1 tablespoon butter or oil

2 eggs

3 ounces cooked Harper's country
ham, sliced very thin

Serves 2

For the eggs Benedict:
In a skillet, heat the oil or melt the butter over medium heat. Fry both eggs until they reach the desired degree of doneness. Keep warm. Heat the ham slices in the skillet until warm.

Split the biscuits and place on a plate. Top each biscuit with a slice of country ham. Top the ham with the cream gravy and a fried egg. Serve hot with Breakfast Potatoes *(see recipe in the Breakfast & Brunch section, page 3)* and freshly sliced tomato.

Blueberry compote

2 cups blueberries

3 tablespoons water

¼ cup sugar

2 teaspoons lemon juice

Lemon soufflé pancakes

1½ cups flour

3½ teaspoons baking powder

1 tablespoon sugar

1 teaspoon salt

1 teaspoon cream of tartar

1 tablespoon lemon zest

1¼ cups milk

1 egg

3 tablespoons butter, melted

Makes 10 pancakes

Lemon Soufflé Pancakes with Blueberry Compote

MAPLE HILL MANOR, SPRINGFIELD ❧ CHEF TYLER HORTON

Maple Hill is located in the heart of Kentucky's scenic Bourbon, Horses, and History tourism region, and is considered by many to be one of the best-preserved antebellum-style homes in Kentucky. These award-winning pancakes are made with a light, lemony batter.

For the blueberry compote:
Combine 1 cup of the blueberries and the water, sugar, and lemon juice in a small saucepan. Cook over medium heat for about 10 minutes. Add the rest of the blueberries and cook 8 minutes more, stirring frequently. Keep warm.

For the lemon soufflé pancakes:
In a large bowl, sift together the flour, baking powder, sugar, and salt. After sifting, add the cream of tartar and lemon zest.

In a separate bowl, mix together the milk, egg, and melted butter. Make a well in the center of the dry ingredients, pour in the liquid ingredients, and mix until smooth.

Heat an oiled griddle or frying pan over medium–high heat. Pour or scoop the batter onto the griddle, using ¼ cup for each pancake. Brown on both sides, creating crispy edges. Serve with butter and warm blueberry compote.

(see photograph on page 1)

3 tablespoons butter

2 tablespoons flour

2 heaping tablespoons
    nutritional yeast

2 tablespoons tamari sauce

2 cups milk

¾ teaspoon dried thyme

½ teaspoon dried sage

¾ teaspoon salt

½ teaspoon black pepper

Makes 2 cups

Snug Hollow Vegetarian Gravy

SNUG HOLLOW FARM BED & BREAKFAST, IRVINE
OWNER BARBARA NAPIER

Snug Hollow serves award-winning vegetarian cuisine, including this meatless twist on sausage gravy. Nutritional yeast adds a flavorful addition instead of sausage and is available in the natural food section of supermarkets or health food stores.

In a medium skillet, melt butter. Add flour and yeast and make a roux by browning the flour and yeast in the melted butter.

Stirring constantly, add the tamari and milk. Season with thyme, sage, salt, and pepper. Cook until thick. Serve over hot biscuits such as Gold Rush Yeast Biscuits (*see recipe in the Breakfast & Brunch section, page 8*).

4 cups oats

1 cup sweetened coconut flakes

1 cup sliced or slivered almonds

2 teaspoons cinnamon

¾ teaspoon kosher salt

½ cup Kentucky sorghum

⅓ cup vegetable oil

2 teaspoons vanilla extract

1 cup assorted dried fruit
    (golden raisins, cranberries,
    cherries, diced apricots)

Makes 7 cups

Sorghum Granola

KENTUCKY PROUD KITCHEN, LEXINGTON
CHEF AND HOST BRIGITTE NGUYEN

Kentucky-based chef Brigitte Nguyen teaches the secrets to "cooking fresh" with products grown locally by Kentucky farmers on the Kentucky Proud Kitchen *cooking show. This granola features a favorite Kentucky sweetener made from the juice of sorghum, a grass that grows prolifically in Kentucky.*

Preheat the oven to 325 degrees. Lightly grease a rimmed 13 x 18 x 1-inch sheet pan with nonstick spray or a light coating of vegetable oil.

In a large bowl, mix the oats, coconut, almonds, cinnamon, and salt.

In a small saucepan over low heat, heat the sorghum and oil to thin the consistency. Remove from heat, stir in the vanilla extract, and pour over the oat mixture; mix well. Transfer to the prepared sheet pan and bake for 40 to 45 minutes. Every 10 to 15 minutes, stir the granola with a spatula so it browns evenly. Remove from the oven and sprinkle the dried fruit over the hot granola.

Using a spatula, flatten the mixture down into the pan (this helps it hold together in clumps as it cools). Cool. Store in an airtight bag or container until ready to serve.

Quiche crust

¾ cup (1½ sticks) cold butter

1¾ cups pastry flour

½ teaspoon salt

6 tablespoons ice water
    (plus 2 tablespoons as needed)

Quiche filling

2 tablespoons olive oil

½ medium onion, finely diced

1 teaspoon salt, divided

½ teaspoon black pepper, divided

1 teaspoon minced garlic

1 pound fresh baby spinach,
    stems removed

6 eggs

2 cups heavy cream

¼ teaspoon freshly grated nutmeg

2 cups shredded Swiss cheese

½ cup crumbled feta cheese

Makes 1 (9½-inch) quiche

Spinach-Feta Quiche

SPOONFUL OF SUGAR . . . SWEETS AND SUCH, MOUNT STERLING
CHEF STEPHEN POWELL

Spoonful of Sugar, a bakery and café, offers homemade quiche on their lunch menu. This quiche, filled with two kinds of cheese and fresh spinach, makes for a satisfying lunch, or dinner. Chef Powell strains the cream and eggs to make sure it is homogeneous without any traces of eggshells or separated egg whites.

For the quiche crust:
Cube the butter into ¼-inch pieces and freeze for at least 1 hour.

Combine the flour, salt, and butter in a food processor. Pulse until the butter is reduced to small pellets. Place this mixture into a large mixing bowl. Add ice water and mix with a wooden spoon until just blended. If needed to bring the dough together, add up to 2 tablespoons more ice water.

Transfer the dough to a clean, lightly floured work surface and knead into a ball.

Cover dough tightly with plastic wrap and refrigerate for 30 minutes.

For the quiche filling:
Heat the oil in a deep, large skillet or Dutch oven. Add the onion, ¼ teaspoon salt, and ¼ teaspoon pepper, and sauté until transparent.

Add the garlic, sauté for 15 seconds, and then add the spinach. Sauté until the spinach is wilted. Remove from heat and chill the spinach. Squeeze the liquid from the cooled spinach and chop into small pieces. Refrigerate again to keep cool.

Preheat the oven to 375 degrees.

(continued on page 16)

Remove the dough from refrigerator. On a lightly floured surface, roll the dough out to ³⁄₁₆-inch thick. Place into a lightly greased 9½-inch pie pan and crimp the edges.

Beat together the eggs and heavy cream. Strain into a bowl and add the nutmeg and remaining ¾ teaspoon salt and ¼ teaspoon pepper. Blend well.

Layer the chopped spinach and Swiss cheese in the crust, starting and ending with Swiss cheese. Slowly pour the egg and cream mixture over the spinach and Swiss cheese. Sprinkle crumbled feta cheese over the top.

Let the quiche sit for 3 to 5 minutes to allow the liquid to seep down into the ingredients. Place on the middle rack of the oven and bake until the filling begins to dome and is firm, 55 to 60 minutes. Cool at least 20 minutes before slicing.

Appetizers & Snacks

Garden Old Fashioned, p. 26

3½ cups flour

2 tablespoons sugar

½ teaspoon baking powder

½ teaspoon salt

¼ cup chilled leaf lard

4 tablespoons (½ stick) butter, cut into thin slices

½ cup cold half-and-half

¼ cup ice water

2 pounds very thinly sliced country ham

Makes about 6 dozen biscuits

Beaten Biscuits with Country Ham

THE GREEN APRON COMPANY, FT. WRIGHT   MAGGIE GREEN

Featuring unleavened dough, beaten biscuits are similar to a thick, tender cracker. Traditionally, beaten biscuit dough is rolled with a biscuit brake. But the only equipment this recipe requires is a stand mixer with a dough hook and a marble rolling pin. Serve with a thin slice of Kentucky country ham and a cold mint julep on Derby Day, or anytime you want to enjoy one of Kentucky's unique snacks.

In a food processor, pulse together the flour, sugar, baking powder, and salt. Add the lard and butter and pulse until the mixture looks like fine crumbs. Add the cold half-and-half and ice water and pulse until the dough clings together. Gather the dough into a ball and wrap tightly in plastic wrap. Refrigerate for at least 4 hours or overnight.

Preheat the oven to 325 degrees.

Divide dough into two parts. Using an electric stand mixer and the dough hook, beat each portion of dough for 4 minutes.

Place the dough on a floured surface. For best results use a marble rolling pin to roll the dough to ¼-inch thickness. Fold the dough in half and roll out again. Continue folding and rolling about six times until the dough is silky smooth and white in color. If you hear the dough pop or snap while rolling, this indicates that it is at the desired consistency. After folding the last time, do not roll out. The dough should be about ½ inch thick.

Cut the dough into circles using a small (1½-inch), round, floured cutter. Place on an ungreased baking sheet. With a three-pronged fork, prick each biscuit two or three times to make six to nine holes. Repeat the kneading, rolling, and cutting with the other piece of dough.

Bake for 5 minutes on the lowest rack. Then move the tray to the center rack and bake for another 20 to 25 minutes, until the biscuits are baked but not browned except just a bit on the bottom. The inside of the biscuit should be dry and flaky when cool. Biscuits can be stored for up to 1 week in a tightly covered container.

To serve, carefully split open the biscuit with a small fork or paring knife. Insert a slice of country ham.

Bourbon-candied ginger

1 cup water

1 cup Kentucky bourbon

2 cups sugar,
    plus 2 tablespoons for dusting

1 cup thin fresh ginger slices
    (peel ginger before slicing)

Ginger onion dip

2 tablespoons olive oil

2 Vidalia onions, julienned

4 shallots, julienned

4 scallions, white part and 1 inch
    of green part, thinly sliced

2 garlic cloves, crushed

1 teaspoon butter

½ teaspoon sugar

¼ cup bourbon-candied ginger,
    finely chopped

1 cup Duke's mayonnaise

½ cup cream cheese

½ cup sour cream

1 tablespoon soy sauce

1 tablespoon fresh lemon juice

1½ teaspoons Worcestershire sauce

¼ teaspoon salt

¼ teaspoon black pepper

Makes about 3 cups

Bourbon-Candied Ginger Onion Dip

BRASABANA, LEXINGTON　　❧　　CHEF JEREMY ASHBY

This dip was created by Chef Ashby as a cross between a crystallized ginger dip his parents served at pool parties when he was young and his other favorite dip, classic French onion. For the best flavors, refrigerate the dip overnight.

For the bourbon-candied ginger:
Combine the water, bourbon, and 2 cups sugar in a pan and bring to a boil. Add ginger, reduce heat, and simmer for 25 minutes. With a slotted spoon, transfer the ginger to a cooling rack. Let dry for an hour and then roll slices in the remaining 2 tablespoons of sugar. Store in an airtight container.

For the ginger onion dip:
In a skillet, heat the olive oil on medium heat. Add the onions, shallots, scallions, and garlic and cook, stirring frequently, until caramelized and golden brown, about 20 minutes. Add the butter and ½ teaspoon sugar and cook for 5 more minutes.

Transfer the onions to a food processor and puree until smooth. Add the bourbon–candied ginger, mayonnaise, cream cheese, sour cream, soy sauce, lemon juice, and Worcestershire sauce and pulse until well mixed. Season with salt and pepper.

Serve chilled or at room temperature with sweet potato chips, pita chips, or traditional potato chips.

2 (6-ounce) cans frozen
   orange juice concentrate

2 (6-ounce) cans frozen
   limeade concentrate

2 (6-ounce) cans frozen
   lemonade concentrate

3 cups water

2¼ cups brewed unsweetened tea

6 ounces Maraschino cherry juice

1000 ml Kentucky bourbon
   (about 4 cups)

Ginger ale

Makes about 20 servings

Bourbon Slush

THE TOUSEY HOUSE TAVERN, BURLINGTON
GABE WAINSCOTT

This recipe was handed down to the Wainscott family by their Grandma Hellman, who lived to the age of 104. At her home, she kept a batch in the freezer for thirsty visitors. Bourbon Slushes are now a popular item on the drink menu at the Wainscott family's restaurants.

In a 12-cup lidded container, mix all the ingredients except the ginger ale. Cover and freeze for 24 hours. Stir the slush several times during the freezing process to break up the ice crystals. Once frozen, the mix can be stored in the freezer for up to 3 months.

To serve, spoon about ¾ cup of the slush into a glass and top with a splash of ginger ale. Serve immediately.

Fig mostarda

1 cup water

1 cup sugar

1 cup dried Mission figs

2 tablespoons butter, cut into cubes

4 ounces whole-grain mustard

2 black peppercorns

1 teaspoon apple cider vinegar

Chicken liver pâté

½ pound chicken livers

1 cup (2 sticks) plus 1 tablespoon
   butter, divided

½ medium onion, diced

½ cup water

1 garlic clove, peeled

1 bay leaf

¼ teaspoon fresh thyme

2 teaspoons Kentucky bourbon

Pinch allspice

¼ teaspoon salt

¼ teaspoon black pepper

Makes 2 cups pâté and
2½ cups mostarda

Chicken Liver Pâté with Fig Mostarda

BLUEBIRD, STANFORD   ✤   CHEF WILLIAM HAWKINS

Chef Hawkins serves fresh, local food at his farm-to-table café, partnering with Marksbury Farm to feature pastured beef, pork, and poultry as well as with other area farms for seasonal produce. The result is delicious food—and a community enriched by sustainable agriculture.

For the fig mostarda:
Combine the water and sugar in a saucepan. Bring to a boil, then turn the heat to low and stir until the sugar dissolves and the mixture is clear, 3 to 5 minutes. Add the figs and bring to a boil. Reduce heat to a simmer and cook for 20 minutes. Remove from heat and stir in the butter, mustard, peppercorns, and vinegar. Let cool.

In a food processor, puree the fig mixture until smooth. Spoon into a glass jar or other airtight container and refrigerate.

For the chicken liver pâté:
Trim sinew, veins, and any gristle from the chicken livers.

In a saucepan, melt 1 tablespoon of the butter. Add the onion and cook until softened. Add the livers and cover with water. Add the garlic, bay leaf, and thyme. Bring to a simmer, cover, and cook until the livers are medium rare and no blood runs out of them when poked with a knife, 5 to 6 minutes. Refrigerate for 2 hours.

Remove the livers from the refrigerator and discard the bay leaf. In a food processor, pulse the livers to chop fine. With the motor running, slowly add the bourbon and mix until smooth. Add the two sticks of butter, 1 tablespoon at a time, blending well after each tablespoon is added. Continue to mix until smooth. Add the allspice, salt, and pepper. Transfer to a crock or jar and cover. Chill until mixture sets; overnight is ideal.

Serve with the mostarda on sliced baguette or canapé toasts.

Cilantro-jalapeño aioli

1 cup mayonnaise

¼ cup chopped fresh cilantro

1 fresh jalapeño pepper,
    seeded and finely diced

1 teaspoon minced garlic

Juice of half a lime

¼ teaspoon salt

Chorizo-Cheddar corn fritters

4 ounces fresh bulk chorizo

1 cup corn kernels

½ cup diced yellow onion

1 cup buttermilk

2 eggs, lightly beaten

2 cups flour

1 tablespoon sugar

1 tablespoon baking powder

2 teaspoons salt

½ teaspoon black pepper

1 cup shredded Cheddar cheese

Vegetable oil for frying

Makes about 25 fritters

Chorizo-Cheddar Corn Fritters with Cilantro-Jalapeño Aioli

BLUEBIRD, STANFORD   ❧   CHEF WILLIAM HAWKINS

Bluebird is one of central Kentucky's premier farm-to-table restaurants. These fritters are a specialty of Chef Hawkins. He varies the ingredients in the batter depending on availability, sometimes substituting chopped country ham for the Stone Cross Farm's chorizo.

For the cilantro-jalapeño aioli:
In a bowl, mix the mayonnaise, cilantro, jalapeño, garlic, lime juice, and salt until well blended. Keep chilled.

For the chorizo-Cheddar corn fritters:
In a skillet, sauté the chorizo over medium heat until browned. Add the corn and onion and cook until soft, about 5 minutes.

In a bowl, combine the buttermilk and eggs.

In another bowl sift together the flour, sugar, baking powder, salt, and pepper. Fold the wet ingredients into the dry ingredients. Stir in the corn-onion mixture and the shredded Cheddar until well combined.

Heat the oil in a heavy pot or deep-fat fryer to 365 degrees. Line a baking sheet with paper towels. Carefully drop the batter by spoonfuls (about the size of a small egg) into the hot oil and fry until brown, about 3 minutes. Drain on prepared baking sheet. Break open one fritter after cooking to be sure the center is cooked. Keep warm in the oven until ready to serve.

Serve with cilantro-jalapeño aioli.

6 eggs

¼ cup mayonnaise

1 tablespoon Dijon-style mustard

2 tablespoons chopped
Housemade Pickles

1 teaspoon Worcestershire sauce

½ teaspoon smoked paprika

Serves 6

Deviled Eggs

HARRISON-SMITH HOUSE, BARDSTOWN
CHEFS NEWMAN MILLER AND JOSH SMOUSE

Homemade mayonnaise and house-made pickles are important ingredients at Harrison-Smith House, especially for their deviled eggs. Substitute store-bought mayonnaise if desired, but don't skimp on the Housemade Pickles (see recipe in the Appetizers & Snacks section, page 27).

In a small pan, cover the eggs with water and bring to a boil. Remove from heat, cover, and let the eggs stand in the hot water for 12 to 15 minutes. Drain and submerge in cold water, then peel the eggs. With a sharp, unserrated knife, cut each egg in half lengthwise and remove the yolks, reserving the whites on a plate.

In a bowl, use an electric mixer to blend the yolks with the mayonnaise, mustard, pickles, Worcestershire sauce, and smoked paprika until smooth.

Spoon the filling into a piping bag and pipe into the reserved egg whites. Refrigerate, covered, until ready to serve.

1 peeled peach slice

2 fresh blackberries

1 teaspoon sugar

Dash Angostura bitters

2 ounces Kentucky bourbon

Splash club soda

Makes 1 cocktail

Garden Old Fashioned

THE TRUSTEES' TABLE AT SHAKER VILLAGE OF PLEASANT HILL, HARRODSBURG ❧ CHEF CLAUDIA HATFIELD

The Shakers were nineteenth-century America's largest and best-known communal society. In 1805, a group of Shakers came to Kentucky and established Pleasant Hill. Kentucky Shakers no longer exist, yet their lasting influence is a legacy to all who visit Shaker Village of Pleasant Hill. This Kentucky bourbon cocktail made with muddled peach and blackberries is a highlight of Shaker Village summer garden dinners.

In a cocktail glass, muddle the peach slice and blackberries with the sugar. Add a dash of bitters and fill the glass with ice.

Pour in the bourbon and add a splash of club soda. Stir and serve.

(see photograph on page 17)

1 cup water

1 cup apple cider vinegar

½ cup sugar

2 tablespoons coriander seed

2 tablespoons mustard seed

1 star anise

1 tablespoon black peppercorns

1½ teaspoons crushed
    red pepper flakes,
    or less if desired

1 tablespoon salt

4 medium cucumbers

1 large white onion

Makes 12 servings

Housemade Pickles

HARRISON-SMITH HOUSE, BARDSTOWN
CHEFS NEWMAN MILLER AND JOSH SMOUSE

Chefs Smouse and Miller base their weekly menu of fine Kentucky fare on the abundance of local meats, fruits, and vegetables raised in and around Bardstown, "the Bourbon Capital of the World." Their attention to serving homemade foods is evident even down to these pickles, which they serve and use in their deviled eggs and other delicious menu items.

In a medium saucepan, combine the water, vinegar, and sugar and bring to a boil. Turn off heat and add the coriander seed, mustard seed, star anise, black peppercorns, red pepper flakes, and salt.

While the vinegar mixture cools (about 15 minutes), slice the cucumbers and onion into a medium bowl. Add the vinegar mixture, covering the cucumber and onion slices. Let cool and store in a clean glass container in the refrigerator for up to 1 month.

❧ **Note:** *You can refrigerate these pickles in a lidded jar, but they're best used within one month.*

Simple syrup

2 cups sugar

1 cup water

Mint julep

1 ounce (2 tablespoons)
   simple syrup

5 to 7 mint leaves

3 ounces Kentucky bourbon

3 ounces water

Ice, crushed or small cubes

Makes 1 julep

Jack's Lounge Mint Julep

JACK'S LOUNGE, LOUISVILLE BAR MANAGER JOY PERRINE

Mint juleps are traditionally served on Kentucky Derby Day in a sterling julep cup or official souvenir glass from the Kentucky Derby. But this frosty drink is just as refreshing all spring and summer long. The Kentucky Colonel variety of mint (Mentha spicata) with its large leaves and spearmint flavor makes a classic julep.

For the simple syrup:
In a small pan over medium heat, heat the sugar and water, stirring until the sugar dissolves. Remove from the heat and let cool. Pour the simple syrup into a very clean glass bottle or jar, label, and refrigerate.

For the mint julep:
Pour the simple syrup into a large glass. Add the mint and muddle well. Add the bourbon and water. Fill with crushed ice or small ice cubes and stir well. Serve garnished with a large sprig of fresh mint. Sip through a long straw.

4 tablespoons (½ stick) butter, divided

3 tablespoons flour

¾ cup milk

½ cup heavy cream

½ teaspoon salt

¼ teaspoon pepper

2 teaspoons minced shallots

1 garlic clove, minced

¼ pound mushrooms, minced

¼ cup finely diced country ham

¼ cup chopped shrimp

2 tablespoons dry sherry

1 egg yolk

⅛ teaspoon freshly ground nutmeg

Pinch cayenne pepper

2 cups kosher or coarse salt

12 fresh oysters

1 tablespoon chopped fresh parsley, for garnish

Serves 4

Oysters Bienville

WINSTON'S, LOUISVILLE ❧ CHEF JOHN CASTRO

Sullivan University and its National Center for Hospitality Studies offer aspiring chefs one of Kentucky's best Culinary Arts and Baking & Pastry programs. Winston's is Sullivan's on-site restaurant where chef-students prepare brunch, lunch, dinner, and desserts inspired by ingredients available in and around Louisville.

Preheat the oven to 500 degrees.

In a saucepan, melt 2 tablespoons of butter. Add the flour and stir to blend well. Whisk in the milk and cream. Allow to thicken and season with salt and pepper.

In another pan, heat the remaining 2 tablespoons of butter. Add the shallots and cook briefly to soften. Add the garlic and mushrooms and cook for about 3 minutes. Then add the country ham and shrimp and cook for 1 minute. Add the sherry, egg yolk, nutmeg, and cayenne pepper. Pour this mixture into the cream sauce and stir. Let cool for a few minutes.

Meanwhile, spread kosher or coarse salt in a thick layer on a rimmed baking sheet or a broiler pan without the rack.

Carefully open each oyster with an oyster knife and set them on top of the salt on the prepared baking sheet. Top each oyster with about 1 tablespoon of the cream sauce (vary the amount slightly depending on the size of the oyster).

Bake until bubbly around the edges, 7 to 10 minutes. Top with chopped parsley and serve immediately.

❧ *Note: Fresh, in-shell oysters can be purchased from any reputable seafood purveyor. Store fresh oysters in a colander with a lot of ice. Put the colander in a bowl to allow the excess water to drain off the oysters. Live oysters are tightly closed. Discard any oysters that are not closed, as this is an indication that the shellfish are dead. When opened, they should have a mild odor, similar to the ocean.*

Smoky ranch dressing

1 cup mayonnaise

Juice of half a lemon

2 tablespoons Dijon-style mustard

1 tablespoon smoked paprika

¼ teaspoon garlic powder

1 dash cayenne pepper

¼ teaspoon salt

¼ teaspoon black pepper

Pickled banana pepper rings

1 (16-ounce) jar pickled banana
    pepper rings (about 2 cups)

½ cup milk

1 cup cornmeal

1 cup flour

½ teaspoon garlic powder

¼ teaspoon cayenne pepper

1 teaspoon salt

½ teaspoon black pepper

Canola oil

Serves 4

Pickled Banana Pepper Rings with Smoky Ranch Dressing

THE GREEN APRON COMPANY, FT. WRIGHT
MAGGIE GREEN

Also popular prepared with fresh-from-the-garden banana peppers, this recipe was inspired by the Fried Banana Pepper Rings served at Smithtown Seafood in Lexington. Fried banana peppers are good as an appetizer or with a fish or chicken dinner.

For the smoky ranch dressing:
In a bowl, mix together the mayonnaise, lemon juice, mustard, smoked paprika, garlic powder, cayenne pepper, salt, and pepper. Refrigerate until needed.

For the pickled banana pepper rings:
Drain the peppers and place them in a bowl with the milk. Set aside.

In another bowl, stir together the cornmeal, flour, garlic powder, cayenne pepper, salt, and pepper.

Heat the canola oil to 350 degrees. In small batches, toss the pepper rings in the cornmeal mixture to coat evenly.

Add the battered rings in batches to the hot oil. They will cook quickly. When browned, remove with a slotted spoon to a baking sheet lined with paper towels. Keep warm in the oven.

Serve with smoky ranch dressing.

Ponzu sauce

½ cup reduced-sodium soy sauce

2 tablespoons brown sugar

2 tablespoons rice vinegar

2 tablespoons mirin (sweet rice wine)

1 pinch crushed red pepper flakes

Pork filling

1 small head cabbage,
    about 1½ pounds

1 teaspoon salt

½ cup fresh cilantro leaves

1 (1-inch) piece fresh ginger

6 garlic cloves, peeled

2 scallions, trimmed

1 tablespoon red miso

1½ teaspoons toasted sesame oil

1½ teaspoons crushed
    red pepper flakes

1½ teaspoons sugar

1 pound ground pork

1 (50-count) package round
    gyoza or pot sticker wrappers

2 tablespoons vegetable oil

3 tablespoons water

Makes 50 dumplings

Pork Gyoza with Ponzu Sauce

MIDDLE FORK KITCHEN BAR, LEXINGTON
CHEF MARK JENSEN

Chef Jensen enjoys working with locally sourced foods to create dishes inspired by world cuisines. These savory gyoza, also known as pot stickers, are always a hit at potlucks and parties.

For the ponzu sauce:
Mix the soy sauce, sugar, rice vinegar, mirin, and red pepper flakes in a small bowl. Stir well to dissolve the sugar.

For the pork filling:
In a food processor, pulse and chop the cabbage until you have 4 cups of a very small dice. Move the diced cabbage to a colander in batches and salt in layers. Set the colander in a bowl and allow time for the cabbage to weep excess liquid.

In the same processing bowl, add the cilantro, ginger, garlic, scallions, miso, sesame oil, red pepper flakes, and sugar. Pulse and chop to form a smooth paste, then mix into the ground pork in a large bowl.

Use your hands to squeeze out any excess water from the cabbage. Discard the liquid. Add the cabbage to the pork mixture and blend well. To test the seasoning, make a small patty with a few tablespoons of the filling. Thoroughly cook it in a small skillet. Taste and add more salt if desired. Keep the raw filling chilled and work with a few cups of it at a time to fill the gyoza wrappers.

To assemble the gyoza:
Lay out eight to ten gyoza wrappers. Place about 1 teaspoon of filling in the center of a wrapper. With your index finger, spread a thin bead of water around the edge of the wrapper. Fold the wrapper in half, cupping the filling in the middle. Working from left to right, repeatedly pleat and pinch the gyoza's edges together until the entire edge is sealed. Lay the assembled gyoza on a sheet pan. (At this point, they can be covered and frozen until ready to cook. Extra filling can also be frozen for another filling session.) Repeat this process until all the gyoza wrappers have been used.

To cook and serve:

Heat 2 tablespoons of vegetable oil in a large skillet with a lid over medium-high heat. Without overcrowding the skillet, place the gyoza, flat side down, onto the oiled hot surface. Let them sizzle and brown. They'll stick to the pan, but do not try to pry them loose. Instead, put 3 tablespoons of water into the pan and quickly cover with the lid. The immediate steam will fully cook the gyoza while releasing them from the pan. When the water has evaporated, the dumplings are cooked (8 to 10 minutes if they are frozen).

Serve with ponzu sauce.

❧ **Note:** *Look for round gyoza or pot sticker wrappers in the frozen or refrigerated section of the international foods aisle of most large supermarkets. Square wonton wrappers can be used as a substitute.*

2 ounces cream cheese, softened

1 (4-ounce) jar diced pimientos, divided

¼ teaspoon kosher salt

¾ teaspoon smoked paprika

¼ teaspoon Worcestershire sauce

1 teaspoon creamy Dijon-style mustard

4 ounces Maddie's Gold or another smoked Cheddar cheese, grated

3 tablespoons thinly sliced scallions, green part only

Makes about 1 cup

Smoked Pimiento Cheese Dip

ED-MAR DAIRY, WALTON CHEF SARA GIBBS

Fourth-generation dairy farmer Eddie Gibson milks his Holstein herd in northern Kentucky and turns it into Ed-Mar Dairy farmstead cheeses. Smoked Maddie's Gold is a Double Gloucester cheese, perfect to pair with pimientos in this classic Kentucky cheese spread, but any smoked Cheddar can be substituted. Bourbon Barrel Foods smoked paprika and Worcestershire sauce both enhance the smoky flavor of this dip.

In the bowl of a food processor, place the cream cheese, 6 tablespoons pimientos with their juice, salt, smoked paprika, Worcestershire sauce, and creamy Dijon. Process until smooth and creamy. Add the grated smoked cheese and pulse until well combined.

Remove to a bowl and fold in the remaining diced pimientos and sliced scallions. Taste and adjust seasonings as needed. Store refrigerated.

Serve with crackers or crudités.

2 ounces Woodford Reserve
Kentucky Bourbon

½ ounce dry vermouth

½ ounce Triple Sec

Lemon twist, for garnish

Makes 1 cocktail

Village Manhattan

THE TRUSTEES' TABLE AT SHAKER VILLAGE OF PLEASANT HILL,
HARRODSBURG   ❧   CHEF CLAUDIA HATFIELD

*Made with Kentucky's own Woodford Reserve bourbon, this classic cocktail
is popular at the Trustees' Table and at Shaker Village's bourbon dinners.*

Place all the ingredients in a cocktail shaker with ice. Shake and
strain into a martini glass. Garnish with a lemon twist.

Pretzel dough

1¾ cup warm water

2 tablespoons sugar

1 tablespoon instant or
    quick-rise yeast

6 cups flour

4 tablespoons (½ stick) butter,
    melted

1 tablespoon kosher salt

¼ cup hot water

To cook the pretzels

10 cups water

⅔ cup baking soda

1 egg, beaten

½ cup Bourbon Barrel Foods
    smoked salt

Makes about 9 or 10 pretzels

Weisenberger Mill Soft Pretzels

HOME CAFÉ & MARKETPLACE, BOWLING GREEN
EXECUTIVE CHEF AND OWNER JOSHUA POLING

*Home Café makes these pretzels only once a year, so they have a cult fol-
lowing. Allow three days to let the dough rest before you make the pretzels.
Enjoy with their recipe for West Sixth Amber Ale Beer Cheese (see recipe on
following page). If you can't find Weisenberger Mill flour, substitute any
unbleached, all-purpose flour.*

For the pretzel dough:

Pour the warm water, sugar, and yeast into the bowl of a stand mixer
and mix well with a dough hook. Let rest for 5 minutes. Add the
flour, melted butter, salt, and hot water. Mix on medium speed until
the dough begins to pull away from the bowl and is smooth, about
5 minutes.

Lightly coat a baking pan with nonstick spray. Portion the dough
into nine or ten 5-ounce dough balls. Evenly space the dough balls
in the prepared pan and wrap tightly with plastic wrap sprayed
with nonstick spray. Refrigerate for 72 hours.

To blanch and bake the pretzels:

Remove the dough from the refrigerator and allow to come to room
temperature (at least 2 hours).

Preheat the oven to 450 degrees.

In a large pot, mix the water and baking soda and bring to a boil.
Roll each dough ball into a rope and then form it into a pretzel
shape. Drop each pretzel into the baking soda water. Cook for 30
seconds, flipping halfway through with a pair of tongs or a chopstick.

Using a slotted spoon, remove the pretzels from the water and space
them out evenly on an ungreased baking sheet. Do not use parchment paper as the pretzels will stick to the paper. Brush each pretzel
with the beaten egg and sprinkle generously with smoked salt. Bake
the pretzels until dark golden brown, 11 to 13 minutes.

West Sixth Amber Ale Beer Cheese

HOME CAFÉ & MARKETPLACE, BOWLING GREEN
EXECUTIVE CHEF AND OWNER JOSHUA POLING

Beer cheese is one of Kentucky's favorite dips. It's so popular, in fact, that Clark County, the birthplace of beer cheese, has developed a Beer Cheese Trail showcasing eight restaurants that each serve their own version of this spicy spread. Chef Poling uses the amber ale from West Sixth Brewing in Lexington for its crisp, malty zing.

In a food processor, beat the cream cheese until very smooth. Scrape the sides of the bowl and add the shredded Cheddar. Blend until very smooth. Add the Worcestershire sauce, hot sauce, garlic, paprika, mustard, cayenne, and salt.

With the processor running, slowly add the beer in a thin stream to blend with the cheese. Use 6 ounces for a thicker, spread-consistency cheese and 10 ounces for a runnier cheese dip.

Refrigerate for at least 24 hours to develop flavors.

Serve with Weisenberger Mill Soft Pretzels (*see recipe on preceding page*) or your favorite crackers and crudités.

2 (8-ounce) packages cream
cheese, softened

2 cups grated sharp Cheddar
cheese, room temperature

1 tablespoon Worcestershire sauce

1 tablespoon hot sauce

2½ teaspoons granulated garlic

2 teaspoons paprika

1 teaspoon dried mustard

¼ teaspoon cayenne pepper,
or more if desired

⅛ teaspoon kosher salt

6 to 10 ounces amber ale,
room temperature

Makes about 2½ cups

8 ounces extra-sharp Cheddar cheese, coarsely grated

2 cups flour

¾ cup (1½ sticks) cold butter, cut into tablespoons

1 teaspoon salt

Rounded ¼ teaspoon cayenne pepper

3 tablespoons milk

Makes about 32 cheese straws

Zesty Cheese Straws

THE MILLER HOUSE, OWENSBORO
CHEF KASEY KIRK-DILLOW

The Miller House was named one of the best fifty-five bourbon bars in the country by The Bourbon Review *magazine. Spirits is the cozy little bar under The Miller House. As a bourbon-focused bar, they have more than 300 bourbons in stock, making them the largest bourbon bar in western Kentucky. These cheese straws are a popular snack item, best served with a cocktail, glass of wine, or iced tea or lemonade. If desired, they can be dusted with coarse salt, seasoned salt, or sesame or poppy seeds before baking.*

Set the oven racks in the upper and lower thirds of the oven and preheat the oven to 350 degrees.

In a food processor, pulse the cheese, flour, butter, salt, and cayenne until the mixture forms a coarse meal. Add the milk and pulse until the dough forms a ball.

Transfer the dough to a lightly floured surface. With a floured rolling pin, roll the ball into a 12 x 10 x ⅛–inch rectangle. Cut dough into 10 x ⅓-inch-long strips with a pizza wheel or lightly floured sharp knife.

Carefully transfer the strips to two ungreased baking sheets, arranging strips ¼ inch apart. (If strips tear, simply pinch the pieces back together.)

Bake, switching the position of the sheets halfway through baking, until the straws are pale golden brown, 18 to 20 minutes. Cool on baking sheets on wire racks, about 15 minutes.

In the remote chance you have leftovers, store them in an airtight container.

Salads & Sides

Sautéed Zucchini with Onion and Peppers, p. 66

4 slices thick-cut bacon, diced

2 scallions, thinly sliced

2 garlic cloves, minced

¼ teaspoon crushed
red pepper flakes

2 tablespoons balsamic vinegar

1 bunch kale, stemmed
and torn into large pieces

Kosher salt and black pepper

Serves 4

Bacon Balsamic Kale

KENTUCKY PROUD KITCHEN, LEXINGTON
CHEF AND HOST BRIGITTE NGUYEN

For this recipe, you can substitute any fresh, leafy green such as Swiss chard, beet greens, spinach, shredded Brussels sprouts, and even romaine lettuce. If using a sturdier green, such as collards or shredded cabbage, cover the pan once the greens have been added and cook until tender.

In a large skillet over medium–high heat, cook the bacon until crisp. Using a slotted spoon, transfer the bacon to a separate dish and remove all but 2 tablespoons of the bacon grease from the pan.

Add the scallions, garlic, and crushed red pepper to the remaining bacon grease and cook for 1 to 2 minutes, stirring constantly. Add the balsamic vinegar and bring to a simmer to reduce slightly.

Pile the kale into the pan and toss it in the hot dressing for 2 to 4 minutes to wilt slightly. Season well with salt and pepper. Crumble the reserved bacon and sprinkle onto the kale. Serve immediately.

Beer Cheese Macaroni and Cheese

GRAZE MARKET AND CAFE, WINCHESTER
CHEF CRAIG DE VILLERS

This macaroni and cheese uses the flavors of Kentucky's favorite cheese dip for its inspiration. Chef De Villers likes to use Country Boy IPA for a rich flavor. He also mixes in Kenny's Farmhouse Cheddar cheese curds and, for more local flavor and crunch, tops the dish with crushed Grippo's chips, made across the river in Cincinnati.

1 pound macaroni or other twirly-shaped pasta

6 tablespoons (¾ stick) butter

½ cup flour

3 cups half-and-half

1 cup India pale ale (IPA)

1 teaspoon dry mustard powder

¼ teaspoon cayenne pepper

¼ teaspoon kosher salt

¼ teaspoon black pepper

Dash hot sauce

Dash Worcestershire sauce

3 cups shredded Cheddar cheese

2 cups (8 ounces) Kenny's Farmhouse Cheddar cheese curds

1 cup crushed potato chips

¼ cup freshly grated Parmesan cheese

Serves 12

Bring a large pot of water to a boil. Add the macaroni and cook until just tender. Drain and rinse with cool water to keep the macaroni from sticking together.

Meanwhile, preheat the oven to 375 degrees. Grease a 13 x 9 x 2-inch baking dish with nonstick spray.

In a large saucepan, melt the butter. Whisk in the flour and simmer, stirring for 1 minute. Whisk in the half-and-half and IPA. Bring to a boil. Whisk in the dry mustard, cayenne, salt, pepper, hot sauce, and Worcestershire sauce. Turn off the heat and stir in the shredded Cheddar cheese, whisking until it melts.

In the prepared baking dish, layer the cooked macaroni with the cheese curds. Pour the cheese sauce over to evenly cover all the macaroni. Stir gently to incorporate the cheese sauce.

Sprinkle the crushed potato chips and Parmesan on top of the macaroni. Bake until hot and bubbly, about 45 minutes. For a crisp, brown topping, broil briefly—watch closely to avoid burning.

2½ pounds russet potatoes
(about 5 medium potatoes)

4 tablespoons (½ stick) butter,
softened

⅓ cup milk

1½ teaspoons salt

¼ teaspoon black pepper

¼ cup Kentucky bourbon

¼ cup heavy cream

1 (5-ounce) package Boursin cheese

Serves 8

Bourbon Mashed Potatoes

AZUR, LEXINGTON CHEF JEREMY ASHBY

*These mashed potatoes make a perfect side dish for Fried Chicken with
Hickory Drizzle (see recipe in the Main Courses section, page 105),
along with the Southern-Style Pole Beans (see recipe in the Salads
& Sides section, page 68).*

Peel the potatoes and cut into chunks. Place the chunks in a large
saucepan and add just enough water to cover. Bring to a boil and
cook until tender, 15 to 20 minutes; drain well and place in a large
mixing bowl.

With an electric mixer, beat in the butter, milk, salt, and pepper until
smooth and creamy.

In a saucepan, mix the bourbon and cream. Bring to a boil, then
lower heat and simmer until the mixture is reduced by half. Beat the
bourbon cream mixture into the prepared mashed potatoes and fold
in the Boursin cheese.

Brussels sprouts

4 cups Brussels sprouts
(about 1¼ pounds)

3 tablespoons extra virgin olive oil

4 teaspoons Old Bay Seasoning

½ teaspoon salt

½ teaspoon black pepper

Manchego cheese sauce

3 cups heavy cream

¼ white onion, peeled

7 garlic cloves, smashed and peeled

2 tablespoons butter

2 tablespoons flour

2 cups (8 ounces) grated
Manchego cheese

½ cup grated Parmesan cheese

1 tablespoon salt

1 teaspoon white pepper

Pinch cayenne pepper

Serves 4

Brussels Sprouts
with Manchego Cheese Sauce

ENOTECA, LEXINGTON ❧ CHEF CARRIE ARPS

This popular wine and bourbon bar on the Kentucky Bourbon Trail features fresh vegetables, including these delectable Brussels sprouts, on their tapas menu. Owners Seth and Renee Brewer recommend pairing this dish with a nice sparkling wine such as a Spanish cava.

For the Brussels sprouts:
Preheat the oven to 375 degrees.

Trim off the stem ends of the Brussels sprouts and remove any loose outer leaves. Cut in half. Place in an oven-safe dish and drizzle with olive oil. Sprinkle with Old Bay Seasoning, salt, and pepper. Toss to evenly coat the Brussels sprouts in the seasoning.

Spread the Brussels sprouts into an even layer and roast until they are toasted and tender, 20 to 25 minutes.

For the Manchego cheese sauce:
While the Brussels sprouts are roasting, set a saucepan on low heat and add the heavy cream. Add the onion and garlic and steep for 20 minutes. Turn off the heat and set aside.

In another pan, melt the butter. Whisk in the flour until well blended and a paste forms. Strain the cream into the flour and butter mixture and whisk until it is steaming and thickened. Turn off the heat and slowly whisk in the cheeses. Add the salt, white pepper, and cayenne pepper.

Place the roasted Brussels sprouts in a serving bowl, pour the cheese sauce over the sprouts, and serve immediately.

Buttermilk Cornbread

WALLACE STATION DELI, VERSAILLES ❧ CHEF ETHAN BOWLING

Housed in a historic country store along scenic Old Frankfort Pike in the heart of Kentucky's Bluegrass horse farms, Wallace Station is known for its panini sandwiches and soups. Cornbread is classic in Kentucky, and at Wallace Station a wedge is served with Whitesburg Soup Beans (see recipe in the Soups & Stews section, page 84).

Preheat the oven to 350 degrees.

Grease a 10-inch cast-iron skillet with bacon grease or butter. Place in the oven to preheat for 15 to 20 minutes until very hot.

Meanwhile, in a medium bowl mix together the cornmeal, flour, baking powder, baking soda, and salt. In a separate bowl, blend together the buttermilk and egg and pour into the cornmeal mixture. Mix well with a whisk.

Using an oven mitt, carefully remove the hot skillet from the oven and pour the batter into the skillet. The batter should sizzle when it hits the pan.

Return to the oven and bake until golden brown, 30 to 35 minutes. Cut into wedges and serve with honey and butter.

1 tablespoon bacon grease or butter

1 ⅓ cups white cornmeal

7 tablespoons flour

1 teaspoon baking powder

½ teaspoon baking soda

½ teaspoon salt

1 ⅓ cups buttermilk

1 egg

Serves 12

4 cups peeled and diced
   butternut squash

2 slices Father's Country
   Hams bacon

4 tablespoons (½ stick) butter

½ shallot, finely diced

¼ cup maple syrup

⅛ teaspoon cayenne pepper

½ teaspoon salt

¼ teaspoon black pepper

Fresh parsley, chopped,
   for garnish (optional)

Serves 4

Butternut Squash with Maple-Bacon Butter

THE MILLER HOUSE, OWENSBORO
CHEF KASEY KIRK-DILLOW

The Miller House has a large garden; the vegetables enjoyed in the restaurant were likely picked that morning. Owner Larry Kirk was four years old when his grandfather took him to Father's Country Hams in nearby Bremen, and he has been enjoying the Gatton family's products ever since, including the bacon for this dish.

In a large saucepan, bring water to a boil. Add the diced squash and cook until soft, about 10 minutes. Drain and set aside.

In a skillet, cook the bacon slices until crisp. Crumble the bacon and drain the bacon grease out of the skillet.

In the same skillet, melt the butter over medium–high heat. Add the shallot and cook until soft, about 3 minutes, being careful not to burn. Stir in the crumbled bacon, maple syrup, cayenne pepper, salt, and pepper. Quickly add the cooked squash cubes and stir to mix with the skillet ingredients. Cook until lightly browned, about 5 minutes, heating the squash throughout.

Garnish with fresh parsley if desired.

1 large head cauliflower

1 cup (4 ounces) grated white
    Cheddar cheese

2 ounces Gruyère cheese, grated

2 tablespoons olive oil

1 medium onion, diced

2 large garlic cloves, minced

½ teaspoon dried thyme

½ cup heavy cream

2 ounces cream cheese

Salt and pepper to taste

½ cup chopped country ham

Serves 4 to 6

Cauliflower Gratin
with Country Ham

ENOTECA, LEXINGTON   &   CHEF CARRIE ARPS

After a bourbon distillery tour, Enoteca is the perfect spot to stop for tapas. This gratin features a blend of cheeses topped with bits of country ham. It pairs well with any Australian shiraz or Spanish garnacha.

Preheat the oven to 375 degrees. Grease an 8 x 8-inch casserole dish.

Remove the outer leaves and chop the cauliflower into small florets. Steam them until tender. Drain and place the cauliflower in the prepared baking dish. Add the Cheddar and Gruyère cheeses and toss until well distributed with the florets.

In a skillet, heat the olive oil over medium heat. Add the onion and cook, stirring occasionally, until softened but not browned, 5 to 7 minutes. Add the garlic and thyme and cook 2 minutes more, stirring constantly. Turn off the heat.

Meanwhile, in a saucepan mix the cream and cream cheese. Whisk over medium heat until steaming and the cream cheese has melted and the mixture has thickened slightly, about 5 minutes.

Add the onion and garlic mixture to the cream and blend well. Add salt and pepper to taste. Pour the mixture evenly over the cauliflower and sprinkle with the chopped country ham.

Bake until bubbly and slightly brown, about 30 minutes. Remove from oven.

Preheat the broiler to high. Return to the oven and broil for a few minutes until the cauliflower is golden brown and the ham is slightly crispy.

Lemon crème fraîche

1 cup crème fraîche

Juice of half a lemon

¼ teaspoon minced garlic
(about 1 clove)

¼ cup chicken stock

¼ teaspoon salt

½ teaspoon black pepper

Chicken livers

Peanut oil

½ pound chicken livers,
cleaned with tendons removed

1½ cups Kentucky Kernel
seasoned flour

Salad

4 cups baby arugula

¼ cup shaved Parmesan cheese,
for garnish

Serves 4

Chicken Livers with Arugula and Lemon Crème Fraîche

HEIRLOOM, MIDWAY   ✎   CHEF MARK WOMBLES

Chef Wombles's secret to preparing delicious chicken livers is to carefully trim the sinew and fatty tissue from each liver and to cook them in a hot, hot pan so the livers come out crisp. The popularity of this dish helped Heirloom get its start. Chef Wombles sources as many ingredients as possible from local purveyors, such as Stone Cross Farm, an approach he also follows at his other venue, Distilled, in Lexington.

For the lemon crème fraîche:
In a saucepan, combine the crème fraîche, lemon juice, garlic, chicken stock, salt, and pepper. Bring to a boil, lower heat to a simmer, and cook until reduced by one-third, about 10 minutes. Keep warm.

For the chicken livers:
Heat 1 inch of peanut oil in a large skillet. Dust the chicken livers with seasoned flour. Sauté in the hot oil until golden brown on both sides. Drain on a baking sheet lined with paper towels. Keep warm in the oven.

To assemble the salad:
Arrange the arugula on a plate. Drizzle with the crème fraîche sauce and top with three or four livers. Drizzle with a bit more crème fraîche sauce and top with Parmesan cheese.

¾ cup plus 2 tablespoons
    (1¾ sticks) butter

16 ounces frozen corn kernels

1 cup plus 2 tablespoons
    cake flour

½ cup cornmeal

¼ cup sugar

1 teaspoon kosher salt

¾ teaspoon baking powder

¼ teaspoon baking soda

½ cup heavy cream

¼ cup milk

1 egg

Makes about 4 dozen

Cornbread Madeleines

DISTILLED AT GRATZ PARK INN, LEXINGTON
CHEF MARK WOMBLES

Located in downtown Lexington in the Gratz Park Inn and along the Kentucky Bourbon Trail, Distilled offers fine dining using local ingredients. The menu explores twists on Kentucky's favorite foods, such as these delicate cornbread madeleines.

Preheat the oven to 350 degrees. Lightly grease madeleine pans with nonstick spray.

In a saucepan, combine the butter and corn and cook until the corn is tender, about 10 minutes. Let cool to room temperature.

Sift the cake flour, cornmeal, sugar, salt, baking powder, and baking soda into a large mixing bowl. Set aside.

In a blender or food processor, puree the corn until it's very smooth. Remove to a bowl and whisk in the cream, milk, and egg.

Stir the corn mixture into the dry ingredients and blend just until mixed.

Using a small spoon, individually fill each madeleine shell about half full. Don't overfill the shell indentations or the cornbread batter will overflow, the shape of the madeleines will be lost, and they will be difficult to remove from the pan.

Bake until madeleines spring back when lightly pressed in the center, 10 to 12 minutes. Let cool for 2 minutes in the pan. Cover the madeleine pan with a parchment-lined baking sheet and invert the cakes out of the pan, or, with a small fork, gently lift each madeleine out of the pan.

Allow to cool before serving. Store in an airtight container.

16 ounces frozen corn kernels

¼ cup diced red onion

2 tablespoons diced fresh
    jalapeño pepper

1 (15-ounce) can creamed corn

1 cup heavy cream

6 eggs, beaten

¼ cup sugar

¼ cup flour

1 tablespoon blackening seasoning

1 tablespoon salt

1 ½ teaspoons black pepper

Makes 10 servings

Corn Pudding

THE VILLAGE ANCHOR, ANCHORAGE
CHEF GEOFFREY HEYDE

*This classic Kentucky dish is served in individual cast-iron crocks at
The Village Anchor. To make at home, use one large baking dish or
cast-iron skillet.*

Preheat the oven to 350 degrees. Grease a 9-inch round cast-iron
skillet or a 13 x 9 x 2-inch baking dish with nonstick spray.

Thaw the frozen corn and press out any excess water. In a large
bowl, add the corn and mix in all the other ingredients.

Pour into the skillet or baking dish. Bake until golden brown
and set in the middle, about 1 hour and 20 minutes.

3 pounds trimmed fresh beets

½ teaspoon salt

⅔ cup sugar

4 teaspoons cornstarch

½ cup apple cider vinegar

2 tablespoons butter

Salt

Makes about 8 servings

Fresh Harvard Beets

CUE ON MAIN, DANVILLE WALLY BREMER

This classic vegetable side dish is a blend of sweet and sour, best savored at room temperature.

Place the beets in a saucepan; add water to cover and ½ teaspoon salt. Cook until tender, about 40 minutes. Reserve and set aside ½ cup of the cooking liquid. Drain the remaining cooking liquid.

When the beets are cool enough to handle, slip off the skins and cut the beets into ¼-inch dice. You should have about 6 cups of diced beets. Set aside.

In a medium-size saucepan, whisk together the sugar, cornstarch, vinegar, and the ½ cup reserved beet liquid. Bring the mixture to a gentle boil. Whisking constantly, cook until thickened, about 30 seconds. Remove from the heat and whisk in the butter until melted.

Stir in the diced beets and cook to heat through. Salt to taste. Allow to cool and serve at room temperature.

Rampch dressing

1 tablespoon canola oil

1 tablespoon mayonnaise

1 tablespoon crème fraîche

2 teaspoons sherry vinegar

2 teaspoons Kentucky sorghum

2 pickled ramp bulbs

Splash of pickling liquid

¼ teaspoon salt

¼ teaspoon black pepper

Country ham crumbs

2 (1-ounce) brioche or
   parker house rolls

2 ounces cooked country ham

4 tablespoons (½ stick) butter

Frisée Salad with Rampch Dressing and Country Ham Crumbs

HARRISON-SMITH HOUSE, BARDSTOWN
CHEFS NEWMAN MILLER AND JOSH SMOUSE

Chef Miller playfully combines ramps with ranch dressing for this popular salad. Also known as wild leeks or wild garlic, ramps grow wild in forested regions of Kentucky. Unlike cultivated onion relatives, ramps have a short season and a unique flavor. This salad pairs ramps with country ham, fresh greens, and deviled eggs for a beautiful representation of spring in Kentucky. If ramps aren't available, substitute shallots or pickled red onion (see Curried Goetta Bowl with Green Tomato Confit recipe in the Main Courses section, page 100).

For the rampch dressing:
In a blender, add the canola oil, mayonnaise, crème fraîche, sherry vinegar, sorghum, pickled ramp bulbs, salt, and pepper and puree until smooth.

For the country ham crumbs:
Cut the rolls into cubes. In a food processor, combine the ham and cubed rolls. Pulse until uniform-size crumbs form.

In a skillet, heat the butter over medium heat, add the ham and bread crumbs, and fry until browned and crispy. Let cool to use as garnish on the salad.

(continued on page 54)

Frisée salad

2 cups frisée or curly endive,
   trimmed and washed

2 cups arugula

1 cup 4-inch-long fresh chive pieces

4 Deviled Eggs *(see recipe in the
   Appetizers & Snacks section,
   page 25)*

Serves 4

To assemble the frisée salad:
Drizzle and massage the frisée with ramp dressing to thoroughly coat.
Add the arugula and chives, season with salt, and place on a plate to
form a nest.

Pipe a fresh deviled egg and set it in the center of the nest.

Finish by dusting the entire salad with crispy country ham crumbs.

Holly Hill Inn's Extra-Creamy Cheese Grits

HOLLY HILL INN, MIDWAY   ❧   CHEF OUITA MICHEL

Holly Hill makes gallons and gallons of grits. This is their counterpoint to Italian polenta and is a delicious side dish for grilled quail, fried or roast chicken, spicy sautéed shrimp, or grilled pork chops. They use stone-ground grits from Weisenberger Mill for a creamy texture. Substitute another cheese for the white Cheddar such as blue cheese, Gouda, or fontina. For an extra rich result, you can also substitute heavy cream for the milk.

2 cups water

2 cups milk

2 teaspoons salt, or more to taste

1 cup stone-ground white grits

2 cups (8 ounces) grated sharp white Cheddar cheese

½ teaspoon cayenne pepper, or more to taste

Serves 4

In a heavy 2- to 4-quart pot with a lid, bring the water, milk, and salt to a hard boil.

Add the grits, reduce heat, and stir until the grits come back to a simmer and start to thicken. Cover the grits and lower the heat as low as possible. At the inn, they cook the grits over very, very low heat for about 90 minutes to let them "swell."

If you don't have this kind of time, cook the grits over very low heat for at least 40 minutes. Stir them occasionally to make sure they don't scorch on the bottom, but don't stir too frequently. When creamy, stir in the cheese and cayenne pepper. Serve immediately.

1 cup warm water

2 tablespoons beaten whole egg

¼ cup sugar

2¼ teaspoons (1 package)
    instant or quick-rise yeast

½ teaspoon kosher salt

3½ cups flour, divided

½ cup butter-flavored shortening,
    melted

1 tablespoon butter, melted

Makes about 3 dozen rolls

Icebox Rolls

THE TRUSTEES' TABLE AT SHAKER VILLAGE OF PLEASANT HILL, HARRODSBURG   ✦   CHEF CLAUDIA HATFIELD

These are some of the softest, lightest dinner rolls imaginable. Leave time to refrigerate the dough overnight.

In a large bowl, mix the warm water, egg, sugar, yeast, salt, and 2 cups flour, stirring until blended. Add the melted shortening and remaining 1½ cups flour. Mix well.

Let rise for 2 hours at room temperature. Press down the dough to deflate, then cover and refrigerate overnight.

Turn the dough onto a floured surface and roll out to ½-inch thickness. Cut rolls with a small round cutter. Brush each round with melted butter and fold over. Put the rounds in 13 x 9 x 2-inch metal baking pans sprayed with nonstick spray and let rise until puffy, about 25 minutes.

While the rolls are rising, preheat the oven to 450 degrees. Bake the rolls until light brown, 10 to 15 minutes. Serve immediately.

1 bunch lacinato kale

5 ounces fresh baby spinach

1 medium Honey Crisp or other
    all-purpose red apple

1 medium red bell pepper, cored,
    seeded, and sliced into
    1-inch strips

¼ small red onion, thinly sliced

1 carrot, shredded

1 cucumber, quartered
    and thinly sliced

1 tablespoon extra virgin olive oil

1½ teaspoons balsamic vinegar

Sprinkle garlic powder

½ teaspoon kosher or sea salt

½ teaspoon freshly ground
    black pepper

1 baguette, sliced

Serves 10 to 12

Kale Salad

RED RIVER ROCKHOUSE, CAMPTON
AARON AND TINA BROUWER

Photographer and self-proclaimed "rock-climbing bum" Aaron Brouwer turned his curiosity for the old Rockhouse into the Red River Gorge's only sustainable-dining restaurant. Aaron transports all the local food himself in his car and makes weekly visits to local farms to pick up ingredients.

De-stem the kale—do not skip this step—by firmly grasping the stem end and, with the other hand, pulling upwards on the kale, removing all the leaf.

Stack four leaves and roll them up like a cigar, then slice into very thin ribbons (chiffonade). Repeat until all the kale is sliced. Place in a large bowl.

Finely chop the spinach and add it to the kale.

Slice the sides off the apple as close to the core as possible without hitting the core. Thinly slice each piece. Stack them on top of each other and cut into matchsticks. Place in the bowl with the kale and spinach.

Mix in the red pepper, red onion, carrots, and cucumber. Sprinkle with olive oil, balsamic vinegar, garlic powder, salt, and pepper.

Serve with sliced bread.

✺ **Note:** *Lacinato kale is also known as dinosaur kale, Tuscan kale, or black kale.*

1 (28-ounce) can pork and beans

3 slices bacon, chopped

¼ cup chopped onion

1 teaspoon dried mustard

¼ cup Moonlite Bar-B-Q Sauce

1 ½ teaspoons brown sugar

Serves 4 to 6

Moonlite Bar-B-Q Beans

MOONLITE BAR-B-Q INN, OWENSBORO
OWNERS THE BOSLEY FAMILY

Starting in 1963, Pappy and Catherine Bosley made the Moonlite Bar-B-Q Inn into a Kentucky tradition by serving delicious mutton and other smoked meats. When I asked the Bosley's grandson Pat for a mutton recipe for this book, he told me (and correctly so), "It's hard to give an exact recipe for smoked mutton. You put the mutton on the smoker and let it smoke. For a long time." What he did share is their barbecue beans recipe, made famous by the addition of their proprietary barbecue sauce.

Preheat the oven to 350 degrees. Grease an 8 x 8 x 2–inch baking dish with nonstick spray.

Pour the beans into the prepared baking dish.

In a skillet, cook the bacon until almost done. Add the onion and cook until the onion is tender. Add the mustard and barbecue sauce and simmer for about 5 minutes. Add the sugar and stir constantly until hot and bubbly.

Pour the bacon sauce over the beans and stir gently. Bake the beans until hot and bubbly, about 45 minutes.

Orange vinaigrette

½ cup orange juice

½ cup white wine vinegar

¼ cup sugar

1 teaspoon salt

¼ teaspoon white pepper

1 egg yolk

1¼ cups canola oil

Asparagus salad

1 bunch asparagus, trimmed

⅓ cup chopped hazelnuts, toasted

Serves 4

Orange Hazelnut-Asparagus Salad

WOODFORD RESERVE DISTILLERY, VERSAILLES
CHEF-IN-RESIDENCE OUITA MICHEL

This salad highlights flavors found in the bourbon-tasting Woodford Reserve Flavor Wheel, such as orange and hazelnut.

For the orange vinaigrette:
In a small saucepan, bring the orange juice, white wine vinegar, sugar, salt, and white pepper to a boil. Cool slightly.

Place the egg yolk in a blender. With the motor running, slowly pour the cooled juice and vinegar mixture into the blender. Then, with the motor still running, very slowly drizzle in the canola oil. The dressing will thicken in consistency and turn very light in color as the oil is added. Refrigerate.

For the asparagus salad:
Steam or blanch the asparagus until just tender and still bright green. Drain well and pat dry.

To assemble:
Place the asparagus spears on a large platter. Dress lightly with the orange vinaigrette and garnish with toasted hazelnuts. There will be leftover vinaigrette. Store chilled to use on salads or for more asparagus.

Bourbon-sorghum vinaigrette

1 cup malt vinegar

1 scant tablespoon salt

½ teaspoon sweet paprika

Dash Crystal hot sauce
  (or other Louisiana-style
  hot sauce)

1 tablespoon grated onion

10 tablespoons Kentucky sorghum

¼ cup Woodford Reserve
  Kentucky Bourbon

½ cup olive oil

½ cup vegetable oil

Grain salad

½ cup wheat berries

½ cup millet

½ cup bulgur

½ cup quinoa

½ cup wild rice

2 ribs celery, small-diced

1 carrot, grated

½ cup small-diced red onion

1½ cups dried cranberries

½ teaspoon salt

½ teaspoon black pepper

Serves 12

Pam's Healthy Grain Salad

WINDY CORNER MARKET AND RESTAURANT, LEXINGTON
CHEF JONATHON TUROCK

*This five-grain salad is a favorite of owner Chef Ouita Michel's mother,
Pam, and is a popular side dish among Windy Corner's patrons.*

For the bourbon-sorghum vinaigrette:
In a large bowl, whisk together the vinegar, salt, paprika, hot sauce,
and grated onion. Warm the sorghum in a microwave oven on
medium power, and then stir into the vinegar mixture along with
the bourbon. Slowly whisk in the oils to thicken the dressing.

For the grain salad:
Cook each grain separately according to package directions. Cool
to room temperature.

In a large bowl, add all the ingredients and mix well. Stir in 1½ cups
of the vinaigrette. Chill at least 30 minutes before serving. Taste for
seasoning and add more salt and pepper if desired. Serve with
vinaigrette on the side.

❧ *Note: For a simpler salad, substitute two and a half cups of any uncooked
  grain for the mix of five grains.*

Peach Jell-O layer

2 (3-ounce) boxes peach Jell-O

2½ cups boiling water

Pretzel crust

3 tablespoons sugar

¾ cup (1½ sticks) butter, melted

2 cups finely crushed pretzels

Cream cheese layer

1 (8-ounce) package cream cheese

1 (16-ounce) carton Cool Whip, thawed

½ cup sugar

1 (28-ounce) can sliced peaches, drained

Serves 12 to 15

Peach Pretzel Salad

CADIZ RESTAURANT   ❦   OWNER SUZANNE HENRY

Served as part of the salad bar every Sunday at the Cadiz Restaurant, this three-layer salad gets rave reviews. In the rare chance that any is left over, it might also appear on Monday's salad bar. Locals line up here for weekly catfish dinners, too.

For the peach jello layer:
In a bowl, dissolve the Jell–O in the boiling water. Cover and chill until slightly thickened, about 1 hour.

For the pretzel crust:
Preheat oven to 350 degrees.

In a bowl, mix together the sugar, melted butter, and crushed pretzels. Press into a 13 x 9 x 2–inch pan. Bake for 15 minutes. Let cool.

For the cream cheese layer:
With a mixer, blend the cream cheese, Cool Whip, and sugar until smooth. Spread evenly over the cooled pretzel crust.

To assemble:
Arrange the peach slices in an even layer on top of the cream cheese. Pour the thickened Jell–O over the peaches. Chill overnight. Cut into squares and serve.

Horseradish cream

1 cup sour cream

¼ cup grated horseradish

Juice of half a lemon

Pinch salt

Latkes

1 large onion, peeled

3 Idaho potatoes, peeled
(about 1 pound)

3 medium parsnips, peeled
(about 1 pound)

3 eggs, beaten

⅓ cup flour

2 teaspoons lemon juice

Peanut oil

Makes about 9 latkes

Potato and Parsnip Latkes with Horseradish Cream

BLUEBIRD, STANFORD   ❧   CHEF WILLIAM HAWKINS

In the heart of central Kentucky, Bluebird proudly serves breakfast, lunch, and dinner using ingredients from the farms and producers around Stanford, such as Root of David nursery and Marksbury Farm. Once grated, the potatoes brown quickly, so follow the steps to keep them from darkening.

For the horseradish cream:
In a bowl, mix the sour cream, horseradish, lemon, and salt. Cover and refrigerate.

For the latkes:
In a large bowl, grate the onion, potatoes, and parsnips. Quickly mix together to coat the potatoes with the onion. This helps keep the potatoes from turning brown.

Place the grated onion, potatoes, and parsnips in a clean kitchen towel. Bunch the towel around the grated vegetables and squeeze the liquid out of the vegetables. Place the grated vegetables back in the bowl and add the eggs, flour, and lemon juice. Stir to form a batter, coating the vegetables.

In a large skillet, heat a ½ inch of oil over medium-high heat. Use a ¼-cup measuring cup to drop batter into the hot oil. Cook on the first side until golden brown, about 5 minutes. Turn and continue to cook until latkes are cooked throughout and browned on both sides, about 3 more minutes.

Drain on a baking sheet lined with paper towels. Keep warm in the oven until ready to serve.

Serve with a dollop of horseradish cream.

Rosemary Braided Bread

SNUG HOLLOW FARM BED & BREAKFAST, IRVINE
OWNER BARBARA NAPIER

This is Snug Hollow's signature bread. The most important step is the six-minute kneading to form a soft, pliable dough.

1½ cups warm water

3 tablespoons active dry yeast

1 teaspoon honey

½ teaspoon lemon juice (optional)

⅓ cup olive oil

1 tablespoon salt

1 cup whole wheat flour

3½ cups or more all-purpose flour

1 egg, beaten

½ cup olive oil

¼ cup chopped fresh rosemary

1 tablespoon chopped or rubbed fresh sage

Makes 1 loaf

In a large bowl, combine the warm water, yeast, honey, lemon juice, ⅓ cup olive oil, salt, and whole wheat flour. Stir well and let rest for about 5 minutes.

Add the all-purpose flour a little at a time, stirring to mix well, until you have a soft dough. Turn out on a floured board to knead.

Knead, adding small amounts of flour as needed, until you have a soft, pliable dough, at least 6 minutes. Pour a little olive oil in your hands and continue kneading until the dough "pops up" when punched. Leave to rest for about 5 minutes.

Preheat the oven to 400 degrees.

Divide the dough into three balls. With your hands, roll each section into a rope about 12 inches long. Braid the strands loosely into a loaf, and pinch and tuck the ends under the braid. Transfer to an ungreased baking sheet and brush with beaten egg. Let rest for 5 minutes in a warm place.

Bake until golden brown, 15 to 20 minutes.

While the bread is baking, mix together the ½ cup olive oil, rosemary, and sage. Set aside.

When the bread is done baking, remove from the oven and pour the olive oil mixture over the hot bread; serve warm.

2 tablespoons olive oil, butter, or lard

1 teaspoon crushed garlic

4 cups diced zucchini

½ red bell pepper, diced

1 small onion, diced

¼ teaspoon kosher salt

¼ teaspoon black pepper

Serves 4

Sautéed Zucchini with Onion and Peppers

NEED MORE ACRES FARM, SCOTTSVILLE
MICHELLE AND NATHAN HOWELL

The Howells are full-time farmers with twenty-five households participating in their CSA. They often have extra fruits and vegetables around to prepare for meals, so in order to keep meals simple, Michelle tends to lean on cooking methods rather than recipes. A good skillet, high-quality extra virgin olive oil (or leaf lard or butter), and kosher salt is often all she needs to turn fresh vegetables into a meal. Substitute broccoli, cabbage, Chinese cabbage, summer squash, Brussels sprouts, or another fresh vegetable for the zucchini if desired.

In a large skillet, heat the olive oil, butter, or lard over medium heat. Add the garlic and cook for 1 to 2 minutes. Add the zucchini, red pepper, and onion and cook for 10 to 15 minutes, or until desired degree of tenderness. Add salt and pepper to taste.

(see photograph on page 39)

Country dressing

½ cup cold water

1 teaspoon dry mustard powder

2 tablespoons sugar

¼ teaspoon salt

2 tablespoons flour

2 egg yolks

¼ cup apple cider vinegar

2 tablespoons butter

Cole Slaw

4 cups shredded cabbage

¼ cup shredded carrot

¼ cup chopped onion

¼ cup chopped celery

½ cup bottled slaw dressing

¼ cup country dressing

¼ cup mayonnaise

¼ to ¾ teaspoon salt

Serves 6 to 8

Shakertown Cole Slaw

THE TRUSTEES' TABLE AT SHAKER VILLAGE OF PLEASANT HILL, HARRODSBURG ❧ CHEF CLAUDIA HATFIELD

Trustees' Table staff take pride in preparing meals with ingredients grown in the vegetable garden just outside the Trustees' Office and from nearby farmers, bringing food from "seed to table." This is one of their most requested recipes, featuring a mix of three dressings for just the right balance of sweet and sour, including a cooked country dressing.

For the country dressing:
Pour the water into a medium bowl, add the mustard, sugar, salt, and flour, and stir until dissolved. Heat an inch or two of water in the bottom pot of a double boiler over medium-high heat. In the top pan, beat the egg yolks and vinegar, then add the dissolved ingredients. Cook and stir the dressing over boiling water until thick and smooth. Stir in the butter. Remove from heat.

For the cole slaw:
In a large bowl, mix all the ingredients together. If the slaw seems too dry, add more country dressing.

❧ **Note:** *For a moist, tender slaw, use the freshest cabbage available.*

2 pounds pole beans

1 smoked ham hock,
    or 1 cup country ham scraps,
    or 6 to 8 slices smoked bacon

2 yellow or sweet onions, quartered

4 garlic cloves, halved

1 bundle fresh thyme

1 bundle fresh sage

1 tablespoon kosher salt

2 quarts water

Serves 8

Southern-Style Pole Beans

AZUR, LEXINGTON ❧ CHEF JEREMY ASHBY

In some parts of Kentucky, this is considered a main dish and not a side dish. Beans are a mainstay of a Kentucky garden. Unlike bush beans, pole beans save space because they grow up a pole, fence, or trellis. The Kentucky Wonder Pole Bean is an heirloom variety of bean; seeds can be purchased or harvested.

Twist the tip of each bean and pull down along the seam to remove the tough fiber, or "string."

In a 3- or 4-quart pot, combine the ham or bacon with the onion, garlic, thyme, sage, and salt. Stir in the water and bring to a boil. Reduce to a simmer and cook for 45 minutes.

Add the beans and cook until tender, 25 minutes.

Scoop the beans from the broth and place in a large serving bowl. Continue to cook the broth until reduced by half. Pour the hot broth over the beans in the serving bowl and enjoy.

1 tablespoon vegetable oil
     or bacon grease

½ sweet onion, sliced

4 medium summer squash, sliced

1 cup half-and-half

¼ cup sugar

¼ teaspoon salt

¼ teaspoon black pepper

Serves 4

Sweet and Scrumptious Summer Squash

POP'S SOUTHERN STYLE BBQ, MOREHEAD
OWNERS LISA AND ADAM FERGUSON

Regional variations in Kentucky's favorite barbecued meat may exist, but fresh-prepared side dishes, such as summer squash, are available at almost all barbecue restaurants across the state. Prepare this side dish in the height of summer when squash fills the garden.

In a large skillet, heat the oil or bacon grease over medium-high heat. Add the onion and cook, stirring, until soft, about 5 minutes. Add the summer squash and cook until barely tender, 6 to 7 minutes.

Stir in the half-and-half and sugar. When it starts to bubble, reduce heat to medium and cook until the sauce is reduced and thickened, about 10 minutes.

Season with salt and black pepper. Serve hot.

Twice-Cooked Thyme Potatoes

THE BLUE RAVEN RESTAURANT, PIKEVILLE
CHEF MATT CORBIN

This recipe is easily doubled. The potatoes can be boiled ahead of time and cooked the second time just before serving. Matt relies on local farmers such as Todd Howard at HF Farms and Cathy Rehmeyer of Four Petal Farm to stock The Blue Raven with fresh Kentucky produce and other seasonal ingredients for his fine Appalachian pub cuisine.

1 pound medium to large
    Yukon gold potatoes
    (about 6 potatoes)

2 tablespoons chopped fresh
    thyme or rosemary

1 teaspoon kosher salt

¾ teaspoon cracked black pepper

1 tablespoon peanut oil, divided

Serves 6

Place the potatoes in a pot large enough to hold them. Cover with cold water and bring to a boil. Cook for 20 to 25 minutes or until the potatoes are done, the skin is still intact, and a sharp knife can be easily inserted into the middle of the potatoes. The potatoes need to remain intact (well short of mashed potatoes). Strain the potatoes and cover with ice water or refrigerate until cooled. (All of this can be done 1 to 3 days ahead of time.)

Once the potatoes have cooled, preheat the oven to 425 degrees.

Place the boiled potatoes on a cutting board. With gentle pressure, press down on the potatoes with your hand until they form a disk. It does not take a lot of pressure. Parts of the middle of the potatoes will be exposed, but the skin will remain mostly intact.

To oven roast:
Place the flattened potatoes on a cookie sheet and season with thyme or rosemary, salt, and pepper. Drizzle each potato with ½ teaspoon oil. Roast in the oven until crispy, 25 to 30 minutes.

To deep fry:
Heat the fryer to 325 degrees. Fry the potatoes in batches until they're golden brown and the skin is crispy. Remove the potatoes from the hot oil and immediately season generously with salt, pepper, and fresh thyme or rosemary.

1 small head cabbage

4 medium carrots

6 ounces brown ale

¾ cup malt vinegar

¼ cup sugar

1½ tablespoons mustard seed

½ teaspoon celery seed

½ teaspoon caraway seed

2¼ teaspoons kosher salt

¼ cup sliced red onion

Serves 6 to 8

West Sixth Beer Slaw

SMITHTOWN SEAFOOD, LEXINGTON
CHEF JONATHAN SANNING

Smithtown Seafood is home to Kentucky's first indoor, commercial-scale aquaponics system. They are also a member of Food Chain, an urban farm that supplies Smithtown with fresh sprouts and other greens. This slaw uses classic pairings with fried cod: malt vinegar and brown ale from the adjacent West Sixth Brewery.

Remove the outer leaves and core from the cabbage. Peel the carrots. Finely shred both and place in a bowl.

Pour the brown ale and malt vinegar into a saucepan. Add the sugar, mustard seed, celery seed, caraway seed, and salt. Bring to a simmer to dissolve the sugar.

Pour the warm dressing over the cabbage mixture. Mix, then cover tightly so the dressing steams the cabbage. Let sit for 1 hour. Stir in the red onion. Mix again and add more salt if desired. Refrigerate and serve chilled.

❧ **Note:** *A one-pound bag of shredded cabbage slaw mix can be substituted for the cabbage and carrots.*

2 heads Kentucky Limestone
    Bibb lettuce

⅓ cup thinly sliced red onion

2 navel oranges, peeled and sliced

1 cup pecan halves, toasted

½ cup crumbled blue cheese

Bourbon-sorghum vinaigrette

Serves 4

Woodford Salad with Bourbon-Sorghum Vinaigrette

WOODFORD RESERVE DISTILLERY, VERSAILLES
CHEF-IN-RESIDENCE OUITA MICHEL

Gagel's Truck Farm supplies Woodford Reserve's restaurant and catering operation with Limestone Bibb lettuce almost year-round. Popular at the Woodford Reserve Bourbon Academy, this salad contains flavors found in the Woodford Reserve Flavor Wheel. The flavor wheel provides flavor notes found in Woodford Reserve bourbon. Dress with bourbon-sorghum vinaigrette (see recipe in the Salads & Sides section, page 61).

Break the leaves from the heads of Bibb lettuce and strip out any tough stems or core. Divide among four salad plates, with the largest leaves on the bottom so the lettuce loosely forms a stack.

Garnish with the red onion, orange slices, pecan halves, and blue cheese. Drizzle with bourbon-sorghum vinaigrette and serve immediately.

Soups & Stews

Bourbon Trail Chili, p. 74

2 pounds ground chuck

¼ teaspoon salt

¼ teaspoon pepper

2 tablespoons olive oil

1 medium yellow onion, chopped

2 green bell peppers, chopped

4 garlic cloves, minced

1 teaspoon dried oregano

1 teaspoon dried sage

½ cup orange juice

3 tablespoons ancho chile powder

2 teaspoons smoked paprika

2 teaspoons ground cumin

½ teaspoon ground chipotle pepper
or minced chipotle in adobo

¼ teaspoon cayenne pepper
(optional, to taste)

1 ½ teaspoons kosher salt

1 (28-ounce) can crushed tomatoes

3 cups water

1 (15-ounce) can or 1 ½ cups
cooked black beans, drained

1 (15-ounce) can or 1 ½ cups
cooked Great Northern beans,
drained

½ cup Woodford Reserve
Kentucky bourbon

Sour cream

Cheddar cheese, grated

Tortilla chips

Serves 6 to 8

Bourbon Trail Chili

GLENN'S CREEK CAFÉ, VERSAILLES   ❧   CHEF PAUL HIEB

This chili is based on flavors from the Woodford Reserve Flavor Wheel. Add bourbon close to the end of cooking so that the alcohol cooks out but the bourbon flavors remain.

Brown the ground chuck in a Dutch oven or soup pot. Season lightly with salt and pepper. Drain off excess fat and set the meat aside.

Add the olive oil to the pan over medium heat, and then add the onion, pepper, garlic, oregano, and dried sage. Sauté until the vegetables begin to soften.

Deglaze the pan with the orange juice. Stir in the ancho chile powder, smoked paprika, cumin, ground or minced chipotle, cayenne pepper, salt, and crushed tomatoes. Bring to a simmer for a few minutes. Stir in the water, beans, and reserved cooked meat. Bring to a simmer again and check the seasoning. Simmer for 15 minutes, add the bourbon, and simmer for 15 to 20 minutes.

Serve garnished with sour cream, Cheddar cheese, and tortilla chips.

(see photograph on page 73)

Pho broth

2 onions, halved

1 large knob ginger, thinly sliced

4 whole cloves

2 pods star anise

1 tablespoon coriander seed

1 tablespoon black peppercorns

1 (2- to 3-pound) whole chicken,
    quartered and skin removed

3 quarts water

2 tablespoons fish sauce

1 tablespoon sugar

Pho bowls

6 ounces rice noodles

2 cups fresh bean sprouts

½ cup fresh mint or basil leaves

½ cup fresh cilantro leaves

2 serrano chile peppers,
    thinly sliced

4 thin slices country ham
    or prosciutto

4 lime wedges

Hot sauce

Serves 4

Chicken and Country Ham Pho

610 MAGNOLIA, LOUISVILLE CHEF EDWARD LEE

Pho is a clear meat broth from Vietnam. This pho contains Chef Lee's favorite Col. Newsom's Kentucky country ham and an abundance of herbs and spices. Roasting the onions and ginger gives the broth a dark brown color and boosts the flavor.

For the pho broth:
Preheat the broiler to high. Place the onions and ginger slices on a small baking sheet lined with aluminum foil. Broil 3 to 4 inches from the heat, turning once, until nicely charred, 5 to 7 minutes. Transfer to a large soup pot.

In a small skillet, toast the cloves, star anise, coriander seed, and black peppercorns until fragrant, about 2 minutes. Add to the soup pot along with the chicken, water, fish sauce, and sugar. Bring to a simmer and cook, skimming the foam from the surface frequently, until the chicken is cooked, about 30 minutes. Remove the chicken to a plate to cool and leave the broth to simmer.

When the chicken is cool, pull the meat off the bones and tear it into shreds. Transfer the meat to a plate, cover, and refrigerate. Return the bones to the broth. Simmer for 1 hour and 15 minutes. Strain the broth through a cheesecloth-lined sieve and discard the bones and vegetables. Add salt if desired.

To assemble pho bowls:
Place the noodles in a heatproof bowl and cover with boiling water for 5 minutes. Drain.

Divide the noodles and broth among four large bowls. Top with the shredded chicken, bean sprouts, mint or basil, cilantro, chile peppers, and country ham. Add a squeeze of lime juice and a few drops of hot sauce and serve.

Homemade croutons

6 slices good-quality bread,
   cut into 1-inch cubes
   (about 6 cups)

2 teaspoons dried thyme

½ teaspoon kosher salt

¼ cup olive oil

Gazpacho

4 pounds ripe tomatoes

1 green bell pepper

1 red bell pepper

1 cucumber

½ cup cubed bread, white part only

6 tablespoons olive oil

2 tablespoons sherry vinegar

2 teaspoons minced garlic

1 teaspoon kosher salt

¼ cup chopped fresh flat-leaf
   parsley or cilantro, for garnish

Serves 8

Gazpacho with Homemade Croutons

ENOTECA, LEXINGTON
SETH AND RENEE BREWER

This gazpacho is a riff on a recipe Seth's mom, Zoe, developed to win second place in a Chex Mix recipe competition. Cucumber and peppers give it a refreshing flavor, and it is silky smooth, not lumpy like many gazpachos. Sourcing summer-ripe tomatoes is a key to success for the recipe.

For the homemade croutons:
Preheat the oven to 350 degrees.

On a large baking sheet, spread out the bread cubes into a single layer. Evenly sprinkle with the thyme and salt. Drizzle with olive oil, toss to combine, and then spread back into a single layer on the sheet pan. Bake until golden brown, about 15 minutes. Set aside.

For the gazpacho:
Remove the core and seeds from the tomatoes and peppers. Remove the seeds from the cucumber. Coarsely chop the vegetables and put them in a blender or food processor along with the bread, olive oil, vinegar, garlic, and salt. Pulse until puréed, then continue to blend until the consistency is very smooth, 4 to 5 minutes (it may be frothy). Season to taste with salt and refrigerate for at least 1 hour.

To serve:
Taste the gazpacho before serving and adjust seasonings as needed. If desired, with a mesh strainer, strain out any remaining seeds or vegetable skin pieces.

Pour into bowls and garnish with croutons and chopped flat-leaf parsley or cilantro immediately before serving.

3 pounds cubed beef stew meat

2 tablespoons vegetable oil

1 teaspoon ground thyme

1 teaspoon ground sage

1 teaspoon ground oregano

1 teaspoon granulated garlic

1 cup diced celery

1 cup diced carrot

1 cup diced onion

1 (12-ounce) can diced
    tomatoes in juice

3 pounds frozen mixed vegetables
    (corn, lima beans, green beans)

1 (7-ounce) can tomato puree

1 (7-ounce) can tomato sauce

1 pound frozen sliced okra

1 tablespoon beef base

1 teaspoon Worcestershire sauce

1 teaspoon lemon juice

1 teaspoon Tabasco™

1 cup sherry

1 cup red wine

1 tablespoon salt

3 pounds Idaho potatoes,
    1-inch dice

8 to 10 cups water

Serves 16 to 18

Keeneland Burgoo

KEENELAND, LEXINGTON ❧ CHEF ED BOUTILIER

Each April and October, the nation's best Thoroughbred owners, trainers, and jockeys converge at Keeneland for the spring and fall race meets. With blooming dogwoods or colorful fall foliage surrounding the limestone walls, a trip to Keeneland is a Kentucky tradition. But the trip isn't complete without a bowl of burgoo or Keeneland's famous Bread Pudding with Maker's Mark Bourbon Sauce (see recipe in the Desserts & Sweet Treats section, page 128).

In a large (12- to 16-quart) stockpot, brown the stew meat in the vegetable oil in batches. Add all the meat back to the pot and brown with the thyme, sage, oregano, and garlic.

Add the remaining ingredients and cover with water. Bring to a boil, reduce to a simmer, and cook until the ingredients have been tenderized but are not mushy, a minimum of 2½ hours. The meat should be fork tender, but the potatoes should hold their shape.

Adjust salt to taste. If too soupy, thicken with a cornstarch slurry.

2½ cups fresh corn
   (from about 5 ears)

1 cup milk

3 tablespoons butter

½ medium onion, finely chopped

3 tablespoons flour

1½ teaspoons salt

¼ teaspoon black pepper

½ cup half-and-half

2½ cups milk

Popped popcorn, for garnish

Serves 6

Popcorn Soup

THE TRUSTEES' TABLE AT SHAKER VILLAGE OF PLEASANT HILL,
HARRODSBURG   ❧   CHEF CLAUDIA HATFIELD

*There's no shortage of recipes featuring corn in Kentucky. This simple
recipe for fresh corn soup uses popped corn as a garnish for crunch
and additional corn flavor.*

In a saucepan, cook the corn in 1 cup of milk until tender, about
5 minutes. Remove to a heatproof bowl.

In the same saucepan, melt the butter, add the onion, and cook
until soft. Stir in the flour, salt, and pepper. Stir in the half–and–half,
additional 2½ cups milk, and cooked corn.

Bring to a low boil and let the soup slightly thicken. Sprinkle with
popcorn and serve hot.

Mint oil

½ cup mint leaves, washed
   and patted dry

¼ cup olive oil

Roasted cauliflower
   and pecan soup

1 medium cauliflower

1 medium yellow onion, diced

2 garlic cloves, peeled

½ cup pecan halves

1 ½ teaspoons salt

¼ teaspoon black pepper

2 tablespoons olive oil

3 cups vegetable stock

½ cup half-and-half or
   unsweetened coconut milk

1 teaspoon fresh thyme leaves

Makes 4 cups

Roasted Cauliflower and Pecan Soup with Mint Oil

THE GREEN APRON COMPANY, FT. WRIGHT   ❧   MAGGIE GREEN

It's not uncommon to find pecans and mint in Kentucky desserts. This unique vegetarian soup features these flavors in a savory soup of roasted cauliflower enhanced with pecans and bright mint oil as a garnish.

For the mint oil:
In a blender, puree the mint leaves and olive oil until smooth. Pour into a small bowl and press a piece of plastic wrap onto the surface of the oil. Refrigerate until the soup is ready to serve.

For the roasted cauliflower and pecan soup:
Preheat the oven to 400 degrees.

Cut the cauliflower into small florets. You should have about 6 cups.

Place the florets on a rimmed baking sheet along with the onion, garlic, and pecan halves. Toss with the salt, pepper, and olive oil. Roast until the vegetables are browned and softened, 20 to 25 minutes.

Place the roasted vegetables in a food processor or blender. Add the vegetable stock and blend until smooth.

Pour into a saucepan and bring to a simmer. Add the half-and-half or coconut milk and fresh thyme. Serve the soup hot, garnished with a drizzle of mint oil.

2 tablespoons olive oil

½ large red onion, diced

3 celery stalks, diced

2 garlic cloves, minced

2 tablespoons smoked paprika

½ tablespoon ground cumin

¼ teaspoon crushed
red pepper flakes

4 cups vegetable broth

2 (15-ounce) cans or 3 cups
cooked black beans, drained

1 (14-ounce) can diced
roasted tomatoes

1 teaspoon salt

½ teaspoon black pepper

Chopped fresh parsley, for garnish

Serves 4 to 6

Smoky Black Bean Soup

THE GREEN APRON COMPANY, FT. WRIGHT   ✆   MAGGIE GREEN

A twist on bean soup, this version uses black beans instead of Kentucky's favorite pinto beans, and adds smoky flavor with Bourbon Barrel Foods' smoked paprika. This soup pairs well with Buttermilk Cornbread (see recipe in the Salads & Sides section, page 44), just like traditional bean soup.

In a soup pot, heat the olive oil over medium-high heat. Add the red onion and celery and cook for about 3 minutes to soften.

Stir in the garlic, smoked paprika, cumin, and crushed red pepper. Cook for 1 minute, stirring. Add the broth, beans, tomatoes, salt, and pepper. Bring to a simmer and cook for 30 minutes.

Garnish with parsley just before serving.

1 pound dried pinto beans

1 cup small-diced white onion

5 ounces country ham, small-diced

2 tablespoons minced garlic

2 teaspoons Worcestershire sauce

2 teaspoons hot sauce

2 teaspoons kosher salt

1 teaspoon black pepper

Serves 4 to 6

Whitesburg Soup Beans

WALLACE STATION DELI, VERSAILLES CHEF ETHAN BOWLING

In the heart of Kentucky's horse country, Wallace Station is on the National Register of Historic Places. The restaurant serves breakfast, lunch, and dinner, along with a weekly chicken dinner and a Friday-night fish fry. They serve gallons of this soup every week. Simple, flavorful, and economical, soup beans are a revered way to cook and eat dried beans. Country ham can be purchased in most supermarkets or from other Kentucky ham producers found in the Sources for Specialty Ingredients section.

Pick over the pinto beans for rocks. Rinse the beans until clean and place in a large stockpot. Cover with 1½ inches of water and soak for 5 to 6 hours.

Place the pot with the beans on the stove and bring to a boil over medium–high heat. Add the onion, ham, garlic, Worcestershire sauce, and hot sauce, but not the salt yet (salt prevents the beans from softening).

Cover and bring to a boil, stirring occasionally. Reduce heat to a slow simmer and cook until the beans change color and are slightly softened but not mushy, about 2 hours. Add the salt and pepper. Taste and add more hot sauce or black pepper if desired.

Serve with Buttermilk Cornbread (*see recipe in the Salads & Sides section, page 44*).

Main Courses

Shrimp and Grits, p. 116

Spice rub

¼ cup salt

2 tablespoons black pepper

2 tablespoons chili powder

2 tablespoons granulated garlic

2 tablespoons dried oregano leaves

2 tablespoons paprika

1 tablespoon ground cumin

Beef short ribs

12 (2-inch) crosswise-cut
     beef short ribs

2 tablespoons vegetable oil

1 carrot, peeled and diced

1 large onion, diced

2 stalks celery, diced

8 cups water

2 cups Bourbon Barrel Ale

2 tablespoons beef base

¼ cup cornstarch

¼ cup water

Serves 6 to 8

Beef Short Ribs with Bourbon Barrel Ale

THE VILLAGE ANCHOR, ANCHORAGE
CHEF GEOFFREY HEYDE

*Braised with Kentucky Bourbon Barrel Ale from the Alltech Brewing &
Distilling Company in Lexington, these short ribs are a tradition on the
fall menu at The Village Anchor. Aged in oak bourbon barrels, Alltech's
ale carries hints of vanilla; in a pinch, you can substitute any amber ale.*

For the spice rub:
Mix all the ingredients together and store in an airtight jar or container.

For the beef short ribs:
Preheat the oven to 350 degrees. Have ready a 3-inch-deep roasting
pan.

Coat the short ribs with the spice rub on all sides. Place on a sheet
pan next to the stove.

In a large skillet, heat the vegetable oil over medium-high heat. Sear
the ribs on all sides until nice and brown.

Place the browned short ribs in a single layer in the roasting pan.
Add the carrot, onion, celery, 8 cups water, Bourbon Barrel Ale, and
beef base. Cover the roasting pan tightly with heavy-duty aluminum
foil to create a seal. Bake for 4 hours. When done, the short ribs
should be fork tender and falling off the bone.

Carefully remove the short ribs to a dish or another pan. Let the
sauce cool slightly and strain to remove the vegetables and excess
fat. You should have about 4 cups of strained liquid.

In a saucepan, bring the strained sauce to a boil. Meanwhile, mix the cornstarch and ¼ cup water in a small bowl. Whisk the cornstarch mixture into the boiling sauce and allow to thicken. To serve, spoon the sauce over the short ribs and plate alongside mashed potatoes or Extra Creamy Cheese Grits (see recipe in the *Salads & Sides* section, page 55).

❧ **Note:** *The short ribs can be prepared a day or two ahead and refrigerated. To serve, remove the fat from the braising liquid, make the gravy, and reheat the short ribs in the oven.*

Beer brine

½ gallon (8 cups) malty beer, such as Against the Grain Brown Note

½ cup kosher salt

½ cup sugar

3 garlic cloves

1 sprig thyme

Half a lemon

½ gallon ice cubes

Chicken

1 (3½ to 4 pounds) whole chicken

2 tablespoons canola oil

½ cup spice rub

Favorite barbecue sauce (optional)

Serves 4

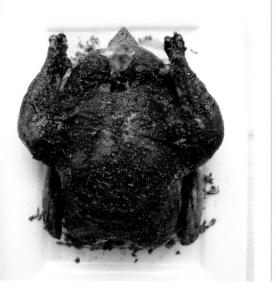

Beer Can Chicken

AGAINST THE GRAIN BREWERY AND SMOKEHOUSE, LOUISVILLE
CHEF JORDAN DELEWIS

A stop along Kentucky's popular Brewgrass Trail, this brewer-owned and operated brewpub offers an exciting and innovative lineup of world-class beers, as well as a fresh and local approach to smokehouse fare.

For the beer brine:
In a large pan, mix the beer, salt, sugar, garlic, thyme, and lemon. Bring to a simmer. Strain into a large bowl and add the ice cubes to lower the temperature of the brine. Put the chicken in the brine to cover. Refrigerate for 12 hours.

To oven roast the chicken:
Preheat the oven to 400 degrees.

Remove the chicken from the brine and rinse under cold water. Pat dry with paper towels and place in a roasting pan. Rub the chicken with oil and sprinkle generously with the spice rub of your choice.

Roast until the internal temperature reaches 160 degrees, about 1½ hours. If the skin begins to brown too much, tent with aluminum foil.

To smoke the chicken:
Preheat the smoker to 250 degrees with offset heat.

Remove the chicken from the brine and rinse under cold water. Pat dry with paper towels. Rub the chicken with oil and sprinkle with the spice rub of your choice.

Place the chicken in the smoker and smoke for about 1½ hours, checking on color after the first 45 minutes to be sure it's browning. Smoke until the internal temperature reaches 160 degrees. If the skin begins to brown too much, tent with aluminum foil.

To serve:
Glaze with your favorite barbecue sauce if desired. Cover with foil and let rest 30 minutes before slicing and serving.

Benedictine

3 ounces cream cheese, softened

¼ cup grated, drained cucumber

2 tablespoons mayonnaise

1 green onion, finely chopped

¼ teaspoon hot sauce

Fried green tomatoes

1 large or 2 medium green tomatoes

¼ teaspoon salt, divided

¼ teaspoon black pepper

⅓ cup cornmeal

⅓ cup flour

1 egg

2 tablespoons water

¼ cup canola oil

Sandwiches

6 strips bacon

4 slices whole-grain bread

Makes 2 sandwiches

Benedictine, Bacon, and Fried Green Tomato Sandwich

THE GREEN APRON COMPANY, FT. WRIGHT ❧ MAGGIE GREEN

Fried green tomatoes are both an early- and late-summer treat in Kentucky, made with unripe red tomatoes. Paired with Benedictine—a cucumber spread made famous by Louisville caterer Jennie Benedict—and crisp bacon, this sandwich brings together three favorite foods of Kentucky.

For the Benedictine:
In a food processor with a metal blade, or using an electric mixer, blend the cream cheese, cucumber, mayonnaise, green onion, and hot red pepper sauce until creamy.

For the fried green tomatoes:
Slice tomatoes into ½-inch-thick slices and lay on a cutting board. Sprinkle both sides with salt and pepper.

In a shallow dish, combine the cornmeal and flour. In another shallow dish, beat the egg and water together.

In a deep cast-iron or other heavy skillet, heat ½ inch of canola oil to 365 degrees.

Dip the tomato slices, one at a time, in the egg and let the excess egg drip off. Dredge both sides in cornmeal. Place the tomatoes in the hot oil, without crowding the pan, and fry on both sides until golden brown. Drain on a baking sheet lined with paper towels and keep warm in a 200-degree oven.

To assemble the sandwiches:
In a skillet, cook the bacon until crisp. Drain and keep warm.

For each sandwich, spread ¼ cup of the Benedictine on a slice of bread. Top with three strips of bacon and two or three slices of fried green tomato. Spread ¼ cup of Benedictine on another slice of bread and place it on top of the tomatoes, Benedictine side down. Gently press the sandwich together with your hand. Cut in half and serve.

Bison meatballs

2½ pounds ground bison

½ yellow onion, chopped

3 garlic cloves, chopped

2 cups panko bread crumbs

⅓ cup (4 ounces) tomato paste

2 eggs

¼ cup heavy cream

1½ teaspoons ground coriander

1½ teaspoons dried basil

1½ teaspoons dried oregano

1½ teaspoons dried sage

1½ teaspoons dried thyme

1½ teaspoons salt

1½ teaspoons black pepper

24 slider or mini-brioche buns

24 thick dill pickle slices

Goat cheese mayonnaise

4 ounces goat cheese crumbles

½ cup mayonnaise

Makes 24 sliders

Bison Meatball Sliders with Goat Cheese Mayonnaise

THE BLUE RAVEN RESTAURANT, PIKEVILLE
CHEF MATT CORBIN

With a seasonal menu that features made-from-scratch twists on Appalachian cuisine, The Blue Raven boasts the best pub food in eastern Kentucky. These sliders feature Kentucky bison as well as housemade pickles. Lean ground beef can be substituted for bison.

For the bison meatballs:
Preheat the oven to 350 degrees. Line two rimmed baking sheets with parchment paper.

In a large bowl, gently mix together the bison, onion, garlic, panko, tomato paste, eggs, cream, coriander, basil, oregano, sage, thyme, salt, and pepper.

Using a ¼-cup measuring cup, shape the mixture into twenty-four portions and place on the prepared baking sheets. Bake until the internal temperature is 140 degrees, about 25 minutes

For the goat cheese mayonnaise:
In a small bowl, use a fork to mash and stir the goat cheese with the mayonnaise. Refrigerate.

To assemble:
After baking the meatballs, toast the slider or mini-brioche buns. Place a meatball on each bun with a pickle slice. Top with the goat cheese mayo and serve.

Bourbon and Coke meatloaf

1 tablespoon butter

1 cup finely chopped onions

¼ cup finely chopped
    celery (1 rib)

1 garlic clove, minced

3 slices thick-cut bacon, diced

1 cup chopped mushrooms

1 pound ground chuck (80% lean)

½ cup fresh bread crumbs
    (from 2 slices bread)

1 egg

1 egg yolk

½ cup ketchup, divided

2 tablespoons Coca-Cola

1 tablespoon Kentucky bourbon

1 teaspoon Worcestershire sauce

¾ teaspoon kosher salt

¼ teaspoon black pepper

½ tablespoon Bourbon Barrel Foods
    soy sauce

1 tablespoon brown sugar

Bourbon and Coke Meatloaf Sandwich with Fried Egg

MILKWOOD, LOUISVILLE   ✌   CHEF EDWARD LEE

These open-faced sandwiches embrace two flavors that made Kentucky, and the South, popular: bourbon and Coke. Also known as poor-man's pâté, meatloaf has its origins in mixing grains into meat to stretch the supply of protein in times of scarcity. Another example is goetta (see recipe in the Breakfast & Brunch section, page 7).

For the bourbon and Coke meatloaf:
Preheat the oven to 350 degrees. Spray a 9 x 5-inch loaf pan with nonstick spray.

Melt the butter in a large skillet over medium-high heat. Add the onions, celery, and garlic and sauté until softened, about 2 minutes. Add the bacon and mushrooms and sauté until soft, another 4 minutes. Let cool.

Meanwhile, in a bowl mix the ground chuck, bread crumbs, egg, egg yolk, ¼ cup ketchup, Coke (or other cola), bourbon, Worcestershire sauce, salt, and pepper. Add the cooled bacon mixture. Mix with your hands until evenly blended and form into a loaf. Place in the prepared loaf pan.

In a small bowl, mix the remaining ¼ cup ketchup, soy sauce, and brown sugar. Brush it over the top of the meatloaf. Bake until the meat reaches an internal temperature of 155 degrees, about 1 hour and 10 minutes. Remove from the oven and pour the drippings into a small bowl to save for the gravy. Let the meatloaf cool for at least 20 minutes.

(continued on page 92)

Black pepper gravy

1½ tablespoons butter

1 tablespoon flour

1 cup reserved meatloaf drippings

½ cup chicken stock

¼ teaspoon salt

1 teaspoon black pepper

⅛ teaspoon fresh lemon juice

Fried eggs

3 tablespoons butter

8 eggs

Sandwiches

8 slices Texas toast

½ cup mayonnaise

8 thick slices tomato

Chopped fresh flat-leaf parsley

Serves 8

For the black pepper gravy:
Melt the butter in a saucepan over medium heat. Whisk in the flour until smooth, then whisk in the reserved drippings and chicken stock. Bring to a simmer, whisking, and simmer for 2 minutes. Add the salt, pepper, and lemon juice. Keep warm until ready to use. The meatloaf and gravy can be made a day ahead and reheated.

For the fried eggs:
In a large skillet, melt a little butter over medium heat. Fry the eggs, two at a time, sunny-side up, for about 3 minutes.

To assemble the sandwiches:
Arrange the Texas toast on a baking pan and toast in the oven until nicely browned, about 6 minutes.

Unmold the meatloaf and cut eight ¾-inch-thick slices from it.

Smear a tablespoon of mayonnaise on each slice of toast. Top with a slice of meatloaf and tomato. Lay a fried egg over each slice of meatloaf. Drizzle with hot gravy and top with chopped parsley. Eat right away.

8 cups fresh broccoli florets,
  or 2 (10-ounce) packages
  frozen broccoli

2 (10-ounce) cans cream of
  chicken soup, undiluted

1 cup Hellman's mayonnaise

1½ teaspoons lemon juice

¾ teaspoon curry powder

2 cups sliced cooked chicken
  (about 2 boneless chicken
  breasts)

½ cup shredded sharp Cheddar
  cheese

½ cup cornflake crumbs or
  dry bread crumbs

3 tablespoons butter,
  cut into small cubes

Serves 4 to 6

Broccoli and Chicken Supreme

GREYHOUND TAVERN, FT. MITCHELL   ❧   GABE WAINSCOTT

This casserole is popular with young and old on the Sunday brunch menu and buffet at the Greyhound Tavern. It is best made with garden-fresh broccoli when available.

Preheat the oven to 325 degrees. Grease a 13 x 9 x 2-inch casserole dish with nonstick spray.

Steam or microwave the broccoli until crisp-tender. Drain well.

In a medium bowl, combine the soup, mayonnaise, lemon juice, and curry powder. Add the sliced chicken.

Layer ingredients in the casserole dish: first the broccoli, then the chicken mixture, then the cheese and crumbs. Dot with butter.

Bake until bubbly and heated throughout, 35 to 45 minutes.

Brussels sprouts salad

2 tablespoons olive oil

1 shallot, thinly sliced

1 teaspoon Dijon-style mustard

1 teaspoon whole-grain mustard

2 tablespoons Kentucky sorghum

1 tablespoon sherry vinegar

3 tablespoons canola oil

2 cups Brussels sprouts

½ cup chopped crisp
    cooked bacon

4 tablespoons pickled red onion
    *(see Curried Goetta Bowl
    with Green Tomato Confit
    recipe on page 100)*

¼ teaspoon salt

¼ teaspoon black pepper

Beer cheese grits

2 cups water

2 cups milk

1 teaspoon salt

1 cup stone-ground white grits

½ cup beer cheese

Catfish with Beer Cheese Grits and Brussels Sprouts Salad

HARRISON-SMITH HOUSE, BARDSTOWN
CHEFS NEWMAN MILLER AND JOSH SMOUSE

Chefs Miller and Smouse serve their wild Kentucky catfish with cheese grits and a refreshing Brussels sprouts salad. They make their beer cheese with white Cheddar cheese and a half-and-half mixture of IPA and Busch Light lager. You can use the West Sixth Amber Ale Beer Cheese recipe (see Appetizers & Snacks section, page 37), simply substituting the white Cheddar and IPA/lager.

For the Brussels sprouts salad:
In a small skillet, heat the olive oil over medium-low heat. Add the shallot and cook very slowly to soften and caramelize, about 10 minutes. Let cool. Whisk in the Dijon mustard, whole-grain mustard, sorghum, sherry vinegar, and canola oil.

Halve and shave all the Brussels sprouts into a bowl. Add the bacon, pickled red onion, salt, and pepper. Toss with vinaigrette and let rest for 10 minutes before serving.

For the beer cheese grits:
Make the beer cheese at least a day ahead of time, using the recipe for West Sixth Amber Ale Beer Cheese and substituting white Cheddar and a blend of IPA and Busch Light lager.

In a heavy saucepan, bring the water, milk, and salt to a boil. Add the grits, reduce heat, and stir until simmering and the grits start to thicken.

Cover the grits and turn the heat as low as possible. Cook over very low heat until thick and very creamy, 35 to 40 minutes. Stir occasionally to make sure the grits don't scorch on the bottom. Keep warm.

(continued on page 96)

Catfish

4 catfish fillets, each split
    into two pieces

½ teaspoon salt

½ teaspoon black pepper

1 cup yellow cornmeal

Canola oil

Serves 4

For the catfish:

Season the catfish fillets with salt and pepper and dust with cornmeal.

In a large skillet, heat 1 inch of canola oil to 360 degrees. In batches, fry the catfish until cooked through, about 3 minutes on each side. Keep warm in the oven.

To assemble:

Spoon the grits into a shallow bowl and top with 2 tablespoons of beer cheese. Follow with two pieces of the fish and finish with the Brussels sprouts salad on top. Serve immediately.

Chicken croquettes

- 2 cups panko bread crumbs, for the filling
- 1 ½ cups chicken broth
- 4 cups diced cooked chicken
- 1 cup sliced fresh mushrooms
- ½ cup (1 stick) butter, melted
- ½ cup finely chopped celery
- 1 tablespoon chopped fresh parsley
- 1 teaspoon finely chopped onion
- ½ teaspoon salt
- ⅛ teaspoon cayenne pepper
- Dash lemon juice
- 2 eggs, beaten
- 2 tablespoons water or milk
- 2 cups panko bread crumbs, for dipping
- Vegetable oil

Mushroom cream sauce

- 3 tablespoons butter
- 3 cups sliced fresh mushrooms
- ¼ cup flour
- ¾ teaspoon salt
- ½ teaspoon black pepper
- 3 cups milk

Makes about 20 croquettes

Chicken Croquettes with Mushroom Cream Sauce

THE TRUSTEES' TABLE AT SHAKER VILLAGE OF PLEASANT HILL, HARRODSBURG ❧ CHEF CLAUDIA HATFIELD

This classic Kentucky dish, made with cooked chicken and fresh mushrooms, is an excellent way to put a traditional spin on leftover chicken.

For the chicken croquettes:
In a bowl, soak 2 cups of the bread crumbs in the chicken broth until the broth is absorbed.

In a food processor, grind the chicken and mushrooms. Add the soaked bread crumbs, butter, celery, parsley, onion, salt, cayenne pepper, and lemon juice. Pulse a few times to mix all the ingredients. Spoon the mix into a bowl and use a ¼-cup measuring cup to shape mixture into 2-ounce croquettes. Refrigerate for at least 1 hour.

For the mushroom cream sauce:
In a skillet, melt the butter, add the mushroom slices, and cook until softened, about 5 minutes. Whisk in the flour, salt, and pepper and stir until blended and smooth. Slowly add the milk, stirring to prevent lumps. Cook until smooth and thickened, stirring constantly. Keep covered and warm over very low heat.

To cook the croquettes:
Mix the egg and water in a shallow bowl. Put 2 cups bread crumbs in another shallow bowl.

(continued on page 98)

Dip the croquettes in the bread crumbs, then into the egg mixture, and then back in the bread crumbs again. This is the secret of good croquettes.

Fry in hot vegetable oil until browned on all sides and hot through–out. Keep warm in the oven.

Top with the mushroom cream sauce and serve warm.

❧ *Note: One three-pound bone-in chicken yields about four cups diced cooked chicken.*

2 cups Brussels sprouts

4 slices thick-cut bacon, diced

1 tablespoon olive oil

1 large onion, diced

1 sweet potato, peeled and cubed

1 cup cubed butternut squash

2 cups chopped kale
    (from about 4 large leaves)

¼ cup balsamic vinegar

Serves 4

Country Boy Hash

BOYCE GENERAL STORE, ALVATON
BRIE AND BRAD GOLLIHER

When Brie and Brad bought a CSA share in Need More Acres Farm, they were overrun with vegetables. One night Brad just started chopping everything and cooked up this hash. It was so delicious that they now make some variation of it almost every night, with Stuartos Fig Balsamic vinegar drizzled on top. They added the hash to their special dinner menus at the store, and it has been a huge hit.

Preheat the oven to 400 degrees.

Trim Brussels sprouts of their outer leaves and cut in half.

In a 9-inch cast-iron skillet, fry the diced bacon in olive oil until well done. Add the Brussels sprouts, diced onions, cubed sweet potatoes, butternut squash, and chopped kale. Cook, stirring, until the onions and Brussels sprout leaves are golden, about 8 minutes.

Press down on the vegetables to squeeze them together. Place the skillet in the oven and bake until the sweet potatoes and butternut squash are tender, 15 to 20 minutes.

Sprinkle with balsamic vinegar and serve immediately.

Green tomato confit

1 large green tomato

1 cup olive oil

½ teaspoon salt

¼ teaspoon black pepper

Curried lentils

2 tablespoons curry paste

1 tablespoon vegetable oil

1 cup brown lentils

4 cups vegetable stock or water

Pickled red onion

1 large red onion

1½ cups water

1 cup apple cider vinegar

1 tablespoon sugar

1½ teaspoons salt

Curry bowls

4 thick slices goetta

¼ cup pickled red onion

1 fresh jalapeño pepper,
    seeded and diced

Fresh cilantro, for garnish

Garam masala, for garnish

Makes 4 bowls

Curried Goetta Bowl with Green Tomato Confit

FORK IN THE ROAD MOBILE GALLEY, LEXINGTON
CHEF MARK JENSEN

This is a multi-step recipe, but once everything is made, the bowls are easy to assemble. Traditional confit uses duck fat, but this version favors olive oil. Prepare the goetta ahead of time following the Goetta (Hog n' Oats Sausage) recipe in the Breakfast & Brunch section, page 7.

For the green tomato confit:
Remove the core and cut the green tomato into very small cubes.

In a small saucepan, heat the olive oil to a temperature of 170 degrees (the oil will be very hot, but not boiling or bubbling). Carefully add the tomato cubes and stir to distribute. The tomatoes should be submerged in the oil. Let them cook for 1 hour, keeping the oil temperature at 170 degrees.

Drain the excess oil and store refrigerated for another confit if desired. Season tomatoes with salt and pepper and refrigerate.

For the curried lentils:
In a small skillet or saucepan with a lid, mix the curry paste and oil. Heat until fragrant. Add the lentils and stir to coat with the curry paste. Add the stock or water and bring to a boil. Reduce heat to medium low and cover. Simmer until the lentils are tender, about 45 minutes.

For the pickled red onion:
Peel and thinly slice the onion. Bring the water to a boil in a saucepan. Add the sliced onion and cook for 1 minute. Drain and set aside the onion. In the same saucepan, whisk together the vinegar, sugar, and salt over low heat until the salt and sugar dissolve. Add the blanched onion and simmer for about 5 minutes. Remove from the heat and let cool. Place in a very clean jar and refrigerate until needed.

To assemble the curry bowls:

When the lentils are almost cooked, heat a little vegetable oil in a large skillet over medium heat. Cook the goetta slices until well browned on both sides and hot throughout. Keep warm.

Line a bowl with curried lentils. Place a warm slice of goetta on top. Top with 2 tablespoons green tomato confit, 1 tablespoon pickled red onions, and a large pinch of fresh jalapeño. Sprinkle with fresh cilantro and garam masala and serve.

Pie crust

1 cup (2 sticks) butter

2 eggs

1 tablespoon sherry or white wine

1 tablespoon ice water,
    plus more if needed

4 cups flour

2¼ teaspoons salt

2¼ teaspoons black pepper

Chicken filling

4 tablespoons (½ stick) butter,
    melted

½ chicken with bones in
    (about 2 pounds)

1 large onion, peeled

1 celery heart (about 6 small
    interior pieces with leaves)

4 large carrots, peeled

4 garlic cloves, minced

½ bunch (5 large leaves) collard
    greens, kale, or Swiss chard

1 cup sherry or white wine

1 tablespoon dried thyme

Double-Crust Chicken Pot Pie

CLEMENTINE'S BAKE SHOP, BEREA
OWNERS LINDSEY WINDLAND AND DREW ELLIOTT

Clementine's menu features baked goods made by hand and from scratch using locally milled flour from Weisenberger Mill. This show-stopping, savory pie builds flavor from the beginning. Lindsey prefers the flavor of sherry in the crust and filling, but white wine can be substituted.

For the pie crust:
Cut the butter into slices and refrigerate. In a bowl, beat the egg, sherry, and water with a fork.

In a second bowl, combine the flour, salt, and pepper. With a pastry cutter, cut in the butter and mix until flaky. Add the egg mixture and stir just until the dough sticks together. Sparingly add more water if needed, 1 tablespoon at a time.

Divide the dough into two balls, one that is two-thirds of the dough and one that is one-third of the dough. Flatten each disk, wrap in plastic wrap, and refrigerate.

For the chicken filling:
Preheat the oven to 350 degrees. Pour the melted butter into a 13 x 9 x 2-inch dish and lay the chicken in the dish.

Chop the onion, celery, and carrots into 1-inch pieces. Mix the vegetables with the garlic, sherry, thyme, sage, celery seed, salt, and pepper. Spread the vegetables on top of the chicken. Bake until the chicken is fully cooked, about 1 hour. After the chicken bakes, strain the liquid out of the baking dish and set aside for the gravy.

Carefully remove the chicken from the vegetable mix. Do not leave any bones. Allow the chicken and vegetables to cool. Pick the chicken meat off the bones. Drain off any remaining liquid and reserve.

Pour the reserved drippings into a saucepan and bring to a boil. Meanwhile, whisk together the water and cornstarch. Add to the

1 teaspoon rubbed sage

1 teaspoon celery seed

1 tablespoon salt

1 teaspoon black pepper

1 cup water

1 ½ tablespoons cornstarch

1 egg yolk, beaten

Serves 6 to 8

boiling drippings, whisking the entire time. Cook until the gravy thickens enough to coat the back of a spoon. Cool and mix the gravy with the vegetables and chicken.

To assemble the pie:
Roll out the larger disk of dough and lay it into a 9- or 10-inch pie pan. Allow some dough to hang over the sides of the pan.

Fill the pie crust with the cooled chicken mixture. Heap the filling so that it is a little taller in the center, as it will bake down some.

Roll out the smaller disk of dough and place it on top of the pie. Seal the crusts by pinching the layers together, creating a decorative edge. Brush the egg yolk on the crust and cut a few slits in the top. Bake until the filling is bubbly and the crust golden brown, about 1 hour. Rotate at least once during baking to brown evenly.

1 pound ground pork

1 pound ground veal

½ pound bacon, ground

1 garlic clove, minced

1 ½ tablespoons kosher salt

1 teaspoon whole yellow
	mustard seed

⅔ teaspoon smoked paprika

½ teaspoon black pepper

⅛ teaspoon ground cardamom

⅛ teaspoon nutmeg

Natural hog casings

Makes about 8 sausages

Fresh Bierwurst

WUNDERBAR, COVINGTON   &   CHEF NATHAN CHAMBERS

Known for their homemade sausages, gigantic homemade pretzels, varieties of mustard, and on-tap German beer, Wunderbar infuses Kentucky with a rustic, fresh German taste. Located in Covington, a city that was once home to an influx of German immigrants, the Mainstrasse area still has a distinctive German feel, complete with a glockenspiel and Goose Girl fountain.

Chill a mixing bowl in the freezer for 30 minutes. By hand, in the chilled mixing bowl, blend all the ingredients except the hog casings. Once blended, refrigerate while setting up the sausage press and casings.

Add the natural casing to the sausage press or casing machine. Tie off the end. Press the sausage mix into the casing until none of the mixture remains in the bowl. Work slowly to avoid air pockets and to fill the casing evenly.

Remove the sausage and remaining casing from the press or casing machine and knot the open end of the casing. Twist into links about the length of your hand. Once all the links are twisted, refrigerate for at least 1 hour to allow the sausage to set and the flavors to develop.

To cook the sausage, boil or grill to an internal temperature of 165 degrees.

& ***Note:*** *Making homemade sausage requires planning and a sausage filler attachment for a stand mixer or meat grinder. For best results, keep all ingredients cold and start with clean equipment.*

Chicken

4 boneless chicken thighs

4 cups (1 quart) buttermilk

1 cup sambal chile paste

3 tablespoons sage

1 teaspoon garlic powder

1 teaspoon ground dehydrated onion

2 tablespoons salt

1 tablespoon black pepper

Hickory drizzle

½ cup hickory syrup

2 teaspoons black pepper

1 teaspoon garlic powder

1 teaspoon ancho chile powder

¼ teaspoon cayenne pepper

Chicken breading

1 cup flour

1 cup potato starch

1 cup finely ground panko
    bread crumbs

2 tablespoons black pepper

1 tablespoon dried sage

1 teaspoon garlic powder

Peanut or vegetable oil

Serves 4

Fried Chicken
with Hickory Drizzle

WILTSHIRE ON MARKET, LOUISVILLE ❧ CHEF JONATHAN EXUM

With its hot and sweet flavor combination and crispy crust, this chicken won the Fried Chicken Throw Down for the Bluegrass chapter of Slow Food USA. For best results, use boneless chicken thighs and coat with potato starch and panko crumbs for a crispy coating. Old Hickory Hill produces hickory syrup on a farm near Owingsville; look for it at local markets or online (see Sources on page 145) If you can't find hickory syrup, substitute a local maple syrup. Chef Exum prefers to buy local chicken from Marksbury Farm.

For the chicken:
Place the chicken thighs in a zip-top bag. Mix together the buttermilk, sambal paste, sage, garlic powder, dehydrated onion, salt, and pepper. Pour the mix into the bag with the chicken and tightly seal the bag. Place in a shallow bowl or dish. Refrigerate for 36 hours.

For the hickory drizzle:
Meanwhile, in a bowl stir together the hickory syrup, black pepper, garlic powder, ancho chile powder, and cayenne pepper. Cover and set aside until needed.

To fry the chicken:
Mix the flour, potato starch, panko, black pepper, dried sage, and garlic powder in a shallow pan.

Transfer the chicken from the marinade to a colander and let drain for 1 minute. Dredge the chicken thighs in the breading. Set aside on a rack for 30 minutes, then dredge the chicken thighs in the breading again.

(continued on page 106)

Heat the oil in a deep skillet to 350 degrees. Fry the chicken thighs for about 9 minutes, checking to be sure the pieces aren't getting too brown. Turn the pieces and continue to cook on the other side until internal temperature reaches 160 degrees, 5 to 8 minutes.

Drain the chicken on paper towels or on a cooling rack and let rest for 5 minutes. The remaining heat in the chicken will bring the temperature to 165 degrees.

Arrange the chicken on a platter, drizzle with the hickory syrup mixture, and serve immediately.

Mint burger sauce

¼ cup mayonnaise

¼ cup sour cream

2 tablespoons chopped fresh parsley

2 tablespoons sugar

1 tablespoon chopped fresh mint

Splash of Worcestershire sauce

¼ teaspoon salt

¼ teaspoon black pepper

Lamb burgers

2 pounds ground lamb

2 tablespoons Worcestershire sauce

1 generous pinch dried mint

1 generous pinch ground coriander

1 teaspoon kosher salt

1 teaspoon ground black pepper

4 large brioche or sweet buns

Cornichons *(see Note)*

Serves 4

Grilled Lamb Burgers with Mint Burger Sauce

GRAZE MARKET AND CAFE, WINCHESTER
CHEF CRAIG DE VILLIERS

Featuring ground pasture-raised lamb from family-operated Colibri Sheep Farm, this generous-size lamb burger, spiked with mint and ground coriander, is worthy of a special occasion. A farm-to-fork restaurant, Graze Market uses as many locally sourced and Kentucky Proud ingredients and food products as possible to create their "blackboard menu," which rotates twice a day depending on availability.

For the mint burger sauce:
Mix together the mayonnaise, sour cream, parsley, sugar, mint, Worcestershire sauce, salt, and pepper. Refrigerate until served.

For the lamb burgers:
Gently mix the lamb, Worcestershire sauce, mint, coriander, salt, and pepper. Shape into four ½-pound burger patties. Grill to the desired temperature—with lamb, medium is best.

Serve on a brioche bun slathered with mint burger sauce and sliced cornichons.

❧ **Note:** *Cornichons (pronounced KOR-nee-shawns) are pickles made from tiny gherkins, a variety of cucumber. They're tart on the tongue, with a hint of tarragon. Look for them in the pickle or condiment section of your local grocer.*

Summer corn salad

4 ears sweet corn

¼ cup chopped fresh cilantro

¼ cup mayonnaise

3 tablespoons fresh lime juice

¼ teaspoon smoked paprika

¼ teaspoon salt

¼ teaspoon pepper

Pickled blackberries

4 cups apple cider vinegar

1 tablespoon mustard seeds

½ cup sugar

¼ cup kosher salt

2 pints fresh local blackberries

2 fresh jalapeño peppers,
   thinly sliced (optional)

Fried okra

2 pounds fresh okra

¾ cup yellow cornmeal

¾ cup flour

¾ teaspoon granulated garlic

⅓ teaspoon dried thyme

2 teaspoons kosher salt

¾ teaspoon black pepper

1 cup buttermilk

Peanut oil

12 corn tortillas

¾ cup crumbled Bleugrass Chevre
   or other local goat cheese

Makes 12 tacos

Kentucky Summer Tacos

HOME CAFÉ & MARKETPLACE, BOWLING GREEN
EXECUTIVE CHEF AND OWNER JOSHUA POLING

Corn, blackberries, okra, and other Kentucky ingredients mingle for this unique vegetarian taco. For the best flavor, prepare and refrigerate the corn salad and pickled blackberries overnight.

For the summer corn salad:
Prepare the grill for medium heat. Grill the corn, turning occasionally, until tender and charred, 8 to 10 minutes; let cool slightly. Cut the kernels from the cobs into a medium bowl. Mix in the cilantro, mayonnaise, lime juice, smoked paprika, salt, and pepper.

For the pickled blackberries:
Bring the vinegar, mustard seeds, sugar, and salt to a boil and stir until the sugar and salt dissolve. Pour the mixture over the blackberries and jalapeños in a bowl. Place in an airtight container and refrigerate overnight.

For the fried okra:
Cut the okra into slices.

Combine the cornmeal, flour, granulated garlic, dried thyme, salt, and pepper in a shallow bowl. Pour the buttermilk into another bowl.

Heat 2 inches of peanut oil in a skillet.

Dip the okra in buttermilk, and then dredge it in the cornmeal and flour mixture. Add the okra to the hot oil in batches and cook until golden brown. Drain on paper towels and keep warm.

To assemble the tacos:
Place a small layer of corn salad on a tortilla, followed by the okra and pickled blackberries, and sprinkle with goat cheese.

Mornay sauce

1 ½ tablespoons salted butter

1 ½ tablespoons flour

1 ½ cups heavy cream

¼ cup grated Pecorino-Romano
cheese, plus ¼ cup extra
for garnish

Pinch ground nutmeg

Salt and pepper

Hot Brown

4 slices Texas toast, crust removed
and sliced in half diagonally

14 ounces roasted turkey breast,
sliced thick

4 slices crisp cooked bacon

2 Roma tomatoes, halved

Paprika, for garnish

Parsley, for garnish

Serves 2

Original "Hot Brown" Sandwich

THE BROWN HOTEL, LOUISVILLE ❧ CHEF JOSH BETTIS

A beloved Kentucky tradition dating back to the 1920s, this now-famous open-faced sandwich is the invention of Chef Fred Schmidt of the Brown Hotel. Made with oven-roasted turkey breast, fresh Roma tomatoes, Mornay sauce, and crispy bacon atop thick Texas toast, the iconic sandwich lives up to the hype. The Brown estimates that more than 1.7 million Hot Browns have been served, and more than 300 are ordered each week, with nearly 1,000 consumed over the Kentucky Derby weekend alone.

For the Mornay sauce:
In a 2-quart saucepan, melt the butter and slowly whisk in the flour until combined to form a thick paste, or roux. Continue to cook for 2 minutes over medium-low heat, stirring frequently. Whisk the heavy cream into the roux and cook over medium heat until it begins to simmer, 2 to 3 minutes. Remove the sauce from the heat and slowly whisk in ¼ cup Pecorino-Romano cheese until the sauce is smooth. Add the nutmeg, salt, and pepper to taste.

To assemble:
For each Hot Brown, place two Texas toast points in an oven-safe dish and cover with 7 ounces of turkey. Take the two halves of a Roma tomato and the remaining two Texas toast points and set them alongside the base of the turkey and bread.

Pour half of the Mornay sauce over the sandwich, completely covering it, and sprinkle with additional cheese. Broil the entire dish until the cheese begins to brown and bubble.

Remove from the broiler and cross two pieces of crispy bacon on top. Sprinkle with paprika and parsley and serve immediately.

Pork Chops Bourbonnais

HOLLY HILL INN, MIDWAY ☙ CHEF OUITA MICHEL

This marinade can be easily halved for a smaller quantity of pork chops. Or make the whole batch, use only half of it, and freeze or refrigerate the other half for another time. Don't freeze or reuse any marinade once it's used on the pork chops.

Bourbon marinade

- 2 cups coarsely chopped onion
- 2 tablespoons bacon grease or canola oil
- ½ cup peeled and coarsely chopped fresh ginger
- ¼ cup coarsely chopped garlic
- 1½ cups apple cider vinegar
- 1 (12-ounce) bottle Bourbon Barrel Ale
- 1 cup Kentucky bourbon, such as Early Times
- 1 cup Kentucky sorghum
- 1 cup brewed coffee
- 1 cup tomato paste
- 1 cup brown sugar
- ½ cup whole-grain mustard
- ½ cup Crystal hot sauce
- ¼ cup Worcestershire sauce
- 1 teaspoon cayenne pepper, or to taste
- 2 teaspoons salt, or to taste

Pork chops

- 12 (6-ounce) or 6 (10- to 12-ounce) bone-in pork loin chops

Serves 6 to 12 depending on the size of the pork chop

For the marinade:
In a large heavy-bottomed pot, sauté the onion in the bacon fat or oil over high heat until it begins to brown. Add the ginger and garlic. Stir frequently to develop a deep caramel color on the bottom of the pot as well as on the onion.

Add the vinegar. Bring to a boil and scrape the bottom of the pot.

Whisk in the remaining ingredients in order and bring to a boil, then reduce to a gentle simmer. Cook over low heat for 1 hour, stirring occasionally.

After cooking, puree in a blender until smooth, in batches if necessary.

For the pork chops:
Place the pork chops in a large baking dish or zip-top bag. Pour in 4 cups of the marinade to coat the chops well. Marinate for 2 hours or overnight (Holly Hill marinates its chops overnight).

Heat a grill to high heat or preheat the oven to 375 degrees. Grill or oven-roast the chops. If you have extra marinade after removing the chops, bring it to a boil in a small saucepan and use it to baste the meat during cooking or as extra sauce at the table.

If grilled, larger chops may have to finish in the oven. Grill them for about 5 minutes on each side, then place in a 375-degree oven for another 10 minutes to finish. Smaller chops are grilled in the same way but do not need oven time.

Store any unused sauce in the freezer or refrigerator for up to 2 weeks.

1 (2½- to 3-pound) pork
    sirloin roast

1½ cups sugar

1 cup salt

½ cup Kentucky sorghum

1½ teaspoons garlic powder

1½ teaspoons onion powder

¾ teaspoon crushed
    red pepper flakes

¾ teaspoon whole coriander seed

¾ teaspoon herbes de Provence

1 bay leaf

Serves 6

Pork Roast with Sorghum Rub

MARKSBURY FARM MARKET, LANCASTER
CHEF WYATT SARBACKER

Rich in salt, sugar, and sorghum, this rub, inspired by a recipe Chef Sarbacker learned from a New Orleans chef, draws out the liquid from the meat, which turns the sugar and salt into a marinade or brine. Chef Sarbacker doesn't serve the pork with any barbecue sauce because it's pretty tasty on its own. If desired, use on pork tenderloin, pork baby back or spare ribs, or bone-in pork chops, instead of the pork roast. The chops, ribs, or pork tenderloin can be grilled for a crispy, browned outer coating.

Place the sirloin roast in a glass baking dish.

In a bowl, mix together the sugar, salt, sorghum, garlic powder, onion powder, and crushed red pepper flakes.

In a spice or coffee grinder, grind the coriander, herbes de Provence, and bay leaf. Stir the ground herb and spice mixture into the sugar mixture.

Coat the exterior of the roast with the sorghum rub. Cover with plastic wrap and refrigerate for 2 days. Every 12 hours, rotate the roast and redistribute the rub. Rotation helps to knock off sugar clumps so they dissolve.

When ready to cook the pork, preheat the oven to 400 degrees. Remove the roast from the refrigerator at least 30 minutes before cooking. Spray a roasting pan with nonstick spray.

Transfer roast to the clean prepared pan. Bake until the internal temperature reaches 145 degrees, 50 to 55 minutes. Brush one time during baking with the remaining marinade to glaze the meat while cooking.

Remove from the oven and let rest for 15 minutes before slicing.

  Note: This recipe makes enough sorghum rub for two small pork roasts, four pork tenderloins, six large bone-in pork chops, or two slab ribs. Store unused rub in an airtight container.

Beef barbacoa

1 (5-pound) chuck roast

2 large onions, peeled

3 medium tomatoes, cored

2 fresh jalapeño peppers

1 whole garlic bulb

1 tablespoon extra virgin olive oil

¼ teaspoon sea salt

¼ teaspoon black pepper

2 dried guajillo peppers

2 dried New Mexico or Hatch chile peppers

2 dried pasilla chiles

1 tablespoon canned chipotles en adobo

1 teaspoon coriander seeds

¼ cup reduced-sodium soy sauce

2 cups orange juice

Tacos

24 corn tortillas

1 large white or red onion, diced

½ cup minced fresh cilantro

¾ cup crumbled queso fresco

8 lime wedges

Makes 3 pounds cooked meat for 24 tacos

Rockhouse Beef Barbacoa Tacos

RED RIVER ROCKHOUSE, CAMPTON
AARON AND TINA BROUWER

The Red River Rockhouse prepares homemade barbacoa from locally raised, grass-fed beef from Marksbury Farm. They prepare forty- to eighty-pound batches at a time, and it's an all-day event. This recipe uses a five-pound roast. From start to eat, it'll probably take about five hours or so, but you'll have plenty to eat now and some to freeze for later.

For the beef barbacoa:
Trim the chuck roast and dust generously with salt and pepper. Preheat the oven to 450 degrees.

Slice the onions and tomatoes in half and place them cut-side down on a baking sheet. Add the jalapeños to the sheet.

Cut the top third off the whole bulb of garlic. Make an envelope with aluminum foil by pulling out a 12-inch piece and folding it in half, then folding the two sides over ¼ inch at a time, to make a tight seal. Place the garlic bulb in the envelope and season with the olive oil, salt, and pepper. Place the foil packet on the baking sheet with the other vegetables, put the sheet pan in the oven, and roast for about 40 minutes. Cool and wipe off any blackened skin on the vegetables. Remove the seeds from the jalapeño. Turn the oven down to 250 degrees.

Meanwhile, in a saucepan cover the dried guajillo, Hatch, and pasilla chiles with water. Bring to a boil and reduce to a simmer until the chiles are soft. Let cool. Wearing gloves, de-stem, deseed, and devein the chiles to remove their heat.

In a small pan over medium heat, roast the coriander seeds until fragrant, about 2 minutes. Grind them to a coarse powder in a coffee or spice grinder.

(continued on page 114)

Squeeze the garlic cloves out of the bulb and drop into a blender or food processor. Add the softened chiles, tomatoes, onions, jalapeños, chipotles en adobo, coriander, soy sauce, and 1 cup orange juice and puree until smooth.

In a Dutch oven, sear the chuck roast on all sides until brown. Cover with the pureed ingredients. Add the remaining cup of orange juice, and water if needed, to cover 90 percent of the meat. Cover with a lid or very tightly with foil and cook until fork tender, 3 to 5 hours. Remove the meat from the pan and set aside until cool to the touch. Save the braising liquid!

Put the Dutch oven with the remaining braising liquid over medium heat and cook until thickened. If the liquid is already reduced (perhaps due to a loose lid), add a bit of water to thin to desired consistency.

For the tacos:
Gently pull apart the beef with forks or fingers. In a sauté pan, add the desired number of tacos worth of beef (about ¼ cup per taco) and 1 tablespoon braising liquid per taco and heat until the liquid is almost reduced. Serve the beef on warm corn tortillas with the diced onion, cilantro, queso fresco, and lime wedges.

Grits cake

3 ¼ cups water

2 tablespoons butter

1 ½ teaspoons salt

¾ teaspoon black pepper

1 cup plus 2 tablespoons
    yellow grits

½ cup shredded Cheddar cheese

⅓ cup blue cheese crumbles

¼ cup chopped cooked bacon
    (about 3 slices)

¼ cup chopped green onion
    (about 2 green onions)

¼ cup flour

¼ cup vegetable oil

Shrimp

1 ½ tablespoons olive oil

3 tablespoons chopped red onion

3 tablespoons chopped
    yellow onion

1 cup sliced shiitake mushrooms

3 tablespoons chopped roasted
    red pepper

1 cup cherry tomatoes, halved

Shrimp and Grits

OTTO'S, COVINGTON   CHEF PAUL WECKMAN

Covington's Mainstrasse Village is home to Otto's, a quaint restaurant that serves up creative dishes in a lovely street-front space. For his shrimp and grits, one of Otto's most popular dishes, Chef Weckman uses a unique combination of shiitake mushrooms, roasted red peppers, and blackening seasoning served over a sautéed cake of cheese- and bacon-infused grits.

For the grits cake:
Grease a 9 x 9 x 3-inch baking pan.

In a saucepan, combine the water, butter, salt, and pepper. Bring to a boil. Gradually stir in the grits and continue to stir until all the water is absorbed and the grits become thick but are still smooth, about 5 minutes. Add the Cheddar and blue cheeses, bacon, and green onion. Stir until thoroughly mixed. While hot, pour the grits into the prepared pan. Refrigerate to cool and allow the grits to set.

For the shrimp:
In a large cast-iron skillet, heat the olive oil over high heat. Add the red onion, yellow onion, and shiitake mushrooms. Allow to caramelize slightly, about 3 minutes.

Add the red pepper, tomatoes, shrimp, capers, and blackening seasoning. Stir to coat, and keep the skillet moving around on the heat.

Once the shrimp is seared on both sides, add the garlic and sauté for 10 seconds. Stir in the wine to deglaze the pan. Allow wine to reduce for about 3 minutes, until slightly thickened.

Remove from heat. Stir in spinach, green onion, and butter. Stir until butter is melted and sauce appears glossy. Add salt and pepper, and adjust to taste.

16 large shrimp, peeled
   and deveined

1 tablespoon capers

1½ tablespoons blackening
   seasoning

1½ tablespoons minced garlic

2 cups dry white wine

1 cup very thinly sliced
   spinach leaves

3 tablespoons chopped green onion

4 tablespoons (½ stick) butter,
   cut into slices

¼ teaspoon salt

¼ teaspoon black pepper

Serves 4

To assemble:

Just before serving, cut the grits into four squares. Coat both sides of each grits cake in flour.

Preheat the vegetable oil in a skillet over medium–high heat. Pan-fry the grits cakes until golden brown and hot, about 3 minutes each side.

Place one grits cake in a shallow bowl or on a plate. Serve covered with the shrimp sauce.

(see photograph on page 85)

2 pounds ground chuck

½ cup chopped onion

½ cup chopped green pepper

2 cups ketchup

2 tablespoons brown sugar

4 teaspoons dry mustard powder

2 teaspoons garlic powder

6 brioche buns

Sliced dill pickles

Serves 6

Sloppy Joe Sandwiches

BOYCE GENERAL STORE, ALVATON
BRIE AND BRAD GOLLIHER

Sloppy Joes are a recipe Brie and Brad started to serve when they first opened the general store. They are made with Downing Cattle Company beef, from Fountain Run, and local onions and green peppers. All summer long, Brie freezes chopped green peppers and uses them each week for this recipe, even into the fall and winter.

In a large skillet, brown the ground beef. Drain off the grease, then remove the meat and set aside.

In the same skillet, sauté the onions and green peppers until soft. Add the ketchup, sugar, mustard, and garlic powder. Bring to a simmer and then add back the ground beef. Cook until warm and bubbly, about 5 minutes.

Serve on a toasted bun with dill pickles.

Chili rub

1 cup light brown sugar

¼ cup kosher salt

¼ cup dehydrated onion

¼ cup paprika

3 tablespoons cracked black pepper

2 tablespoons ancho chile powder

2 tablespoons granulated garlic

2 tablespoons mace

2 tablespoons dry mustard powder

1 tablespoon cayenne pepper

2 teaspoons ground cumin

2 teaspoons ground coriander

Bourbon-peppercorn barbecue sauce

2 tablespoons vegetable oil

1 pound sweet Vidalia onions (about 2 medium onions), finely diced

6 garlic cloves, minced

3 cups Kentucky bourbon, divided

1½ pounds light brown sugar

2 cups finely diced roasted red bell pepper

1½ cups Worcestershire sauce

8 cups (64 ounces) Heinz ketchup

Smoked Pork Shoulder with Chili Rub and Bourbon-Peppercorn Barbecue Sauce

WILTSHIRE PANTRY, LOUISVILLE   ❧   CHEF REED JOHNSON

Born in western Kentucky, Chef Johnson knows barbecue. He prefers the indirect heat of a wood-burning offset smoker and pays close attention to the dampers (and thermometer readings) to produce perfectly smoked pork. As Reed says, "Smoking meat takes awhile. Have the family over . . . embrace around the smoke-filled atmosphere. It's a magical event."

For the chili rub:
In a medium bowl, sift all the ingredients together until well mixed. Unused rub can be shelved at room temperature in an airtight container.

For the bourbon-peppercorn barbecue sauce:
In a 6-quart pan, heat the vegetable oil. Cook the onion and garlic until translucent, about 5 minutes. Add 2 cups of bourbon, being very careful—the alcohol may ignite, particularly if using a shallow pan over a gas flame. Cook for about 2 minutes, and then add the brown sugar and red pepper. Stir until the sugar dissolves. Stir in the Worcestershire sauce, ketchup, and cider vinegar. Simmer for 10 minutes.

Add the black pepper, salt, and lemon juice, reduce to low heat, and simmer for 1 hour, stirring every 15 minutes. Remove from heat and stir in the remaining cup of bourbon. Puree for a smoother sauce if desired.

For the pork shoulder:
Trim excess fat from the pork shoulder, leaving a ⅛- to ¼-inch fat cap all around. Mix the vegetable oil and mustard and work it into the pork with your hands. Then massage the chili rub into the pork, into

4 cups (32 ounces) apple cider
   vinegar

2 tablespoons coarsely ground
   black pepper

¼ cup kosher salt

2 tablespoons lemon juice

Pork shoulder

1 (6- to 8-pound) pork shoulder
   or Boston butt

¼ cup vegetable oil

¼ cup Dijon-style mustard

Serves 15

every crack. It's called rub for a reason! Cover and refrigerate the pork; let rest for up to 24 hours (but no less than 2 hours). Bring the pork to room temperature for an hour before putting it in the smoker.

In a smoker or grill *(see Note)*, build a fire with hardwood lump charcoal, allowing time for a good base of gray coals to form. Use wild cherry or green shagbark hickory for smoke (apple, peach, or oak are good, too). Start with a big chunk or two laid directly on the coals. If using wood chips, soak them in water, wrap them in foil, poke fork holes in the foil, and place the packet on the coals. For the best flavor, don't use old wood. Add wood for smoking every couple of hours.

When the smoker holds a steady 225 to 250 degrees and is thick with smoke, add the pork. Every 1 to 2 hours, check if more wood or charcoal is needed; adjust the dampers for a steady temperature and smokiness. Rotate the pork for even cooking.

After 6 hours, check the internal temperature of the pork with a thermometer. Smoke the pork to an internal temperature of 160 degrees, then remove it from the smoker and wrap tightly in heavy-duty foil. Put the wrapped pork back in the smoker (or in a 250-degree oven) and cook to an internal temperature of 195 to 205 degrees. Remove the pork and let rest for at least an hour before opening the foil.

When ready to serve, open the foil. The pork should pull apart freely with your hands, tongs, or forks. Serve the shredded pork on a platter with bourbon-peppercorn barbecue sauce on the side.

  Note: *If using a grill, build your fire on one side. Place a pan of water over the heat and smoke the pork on the other side. This is smoking, not grilling. Also, don't use charcoal infused with starter fluid—it imparts an unpleasant flavor.*

1 pound Arborio rice

6 cups mushroom or beef stock

1⅓ cups quartered shiitake
   mushrooms

¼ cup extra virgin olive oil

4 tablespoons (½ stick) butter

½ cup shredded Parmesan
   cheese, plus more for garnish

1 teaspoon salt

1 teaspoon black pepper

Serves 8

Wild Mushroom Risotto

THE VILLAGE ANCHOR, ANCHORAGE
OWNER KEVIN GRANGIER ❧ CHEF GEOFFREY HEYDE

A favorite vegetarian dish of The Village Anchor customers, this risotto can be made with Kentucky-grown shiitake mushrooms from Sheltowee Farm.

In a saucepan over medium-low heat, toast the Arborio rice lightly until it has a nutty aroma, being careful not to burn.

In another saucepan, bring the 6 cups stock to a boil. During the risotto-making process, keep the stock hot.

With a ladle or heatproof measuring cup, add 2 cups of the boiling stock to the rice, stirring constantly until all the liquid is absorbed. Repeat with another 2 cups of boiling stock. When all the liquid is absorbed, add the final 2 cups of boiling stock and the quartered mushrooms. Once almost all the liquid is absorbed, stir in the olive oil, butter, cheese, salt, and pepper.

Serve hot with additional shredded Parmesan cheese for a garnish.

Desserts & Sweet Treats

Lemon Bars, p. 139

Blackberry jam cupcakes

4 cups flour

¾ teaspoon baking soda

1½ teaspoons cinnamon

¼ teaspoon ground cloves

1 cup (2 sticks) butter

2 cups sugar

4 eggs

1½ cups seedless blackberry jam

¾ cup buttermilk

Soft caramel frosting

6 tablespoons (¾ stick) butter

1 cup brown sugar

3 tablespoons milk

1¾ cups powdered sugar

15 fresh blackberries

¼ cup granulated sugar

Makes 15 jumbo-size
(2¼-inch) cupcakes

Blackberry Jam Cupcakes

THE GREEN APRON COMPANY, FT. WRIGHT   ❧   MAGGIE GREEN

Blackberry jam cake is a Kentucky favorite. These cupcakes are based on my grandmother's jam cake recipe. I like to bake with a lower oven temperature to ensure that the cupcakes fully cook without the edges getting too brown. To keep the frosting soft, be sure not to cook the brown sugar and butter too long and don't let it boil. It also might seem like you need to mix in additional powdered sugar to thicken the icing, but don't do so. The frosting thickens as it cools.

Preheat the oven to 300 degrees. Line a jumbo cupcake pan with large cupcake papers.

For the blackberry jam cupcakes:
In a large bowl, whisk together the flour, baking soda, cinnamon, and ground cloves.

With an electric mixer, cream the butter and sugar until light and fluffy, at least 5 minutes. Add the eggs, one at a time, beating well after each addition. Mix in the jam. Add the flour and spice mixture to the creamed butter mixture, alternating with the buttermilk and beginning and ending with the flour.

Fill cupcake liners three-fourths full with batter. Bake until a toothpick inserted in the center comes out clean, about 33 to 35 minutes. Let the cupcakes cool in pans for 5 minutes, and then remove to wire racks to finish cooling.

For the soft caramel frosting:
In a saucepan, melt the butter over low heat. Turn off the heat and mix in the brown sugar and milk until the brown sugar is dissolved and the mixture is smooth. With a mixer, stir in the powdered sugar and beat until smooth. The frosting will set up as it cools. Once the cupcakes are cool, spread with the frosting. Roll the blackberries in granulated sugar and garnish each cupcake with a sugared blackberry.

Chocolate layer cake

2 cups sugar

1¾ cups flour

¾ cup cocoa

1½ teaspoons baking powder

1½ teaspoons baking soda

1 teaspoon salt

2 eggs

1 cup buttermilk

½ cup vegetable oil

1 cup hot coffee

Bourbon buttercream frosting

1 cup (2 sticks) butter,
        at room temperature

4 cups powdered sugar

3 to 4 tablespoons Bulleit
        bourbon (or more!)

1 teaspoon vanilla extract

Makes 1 (9-inch) round cake

Bourbon Ball Layer Cake

CLEMENTINE'S BAKE SHOP, BEREA
OWNERS LINDSEY WINDLAND AND DREW ELLIOTT

With a moist chocolate interior and a bourbon-spiked buttercream frosting, this layer cake is a clever twist on bourbon ball candy, a favorite Kentucky treat.

Preheat the oven to 350 degrees.

For the chocolate layer cake:
Grease and flour three 9-inch round pans and line them with parchment paper.

In a large mixing bowl, stir in the sugar, flour, cocoa, baking powder, baking soda, and salt.

Add eggs, buttermilk, and oil. Beat on medium speed for about 2 minutes. Stir in hot coffee. The batter will be very thin.

Divide evenly between the three prepared pans. Bake until a toothpick inserted in the center comes out clean, 22 to 25 minutes.

Cool for about 10 minutes. Run a thin knife around the edge of each pan. Carefully turn the cakes out of the pans onto a cooling rack. (If the cake doesn't fall from the pan, tap the bottom of the pan until the cake is released.) Allow to cool. Remove the parchment paper.

For the bourbon buttercream frosting:
With an electric mixer, cream the butter until light and fluffy. Add the powdered sugar 1 cup at a time, adding bourbon in between each addition. Scrape the sides of the bowl, add vanilla, and whip on high for 45 seconds. Sandwich the frosting between the cake layers, saving enough to frost the sides and top of the cake.

Butter pie crust

1¾ cups flour

½ teaspoon salt

¾ cup (1½ sticks) cold butter

6 tablespoons ice water

Bourbon pecan pie filling

1 cup sugar

3 tablespoons butter, melted

½ cup dark corn syrup

3 eggs, beaten

1½ to 2 cups pecan halves

2 tablespoons Kentucky bourbon

Makes 1 (9-inch) pie

Bourbon Pecan Pie

BOURBON MANOR BED & BREAKFAST, BARDSTOWN
CHEF TYLER HORTON

The flavor of Kentucky bourbon enriches this take on a classic Kentucky dessert. Bourbon Manor, nestled in the heart of Bardstown, Kentucky's bourbon capital, is a perfect place to spend the night along the Kentucky Bourbon Trail.

For the butter pie crust:
In a food processor bowl, mix the flour and salt. Cut the butter into slices and add it to the flour. Pulse about 20 times to cut in the butter so it looks like coarse bread crumbs. Add the ice water all at once. Pulse again just until the dough forms a ball. Remove from the processor, wrap in plastic wrap, and refrigerate for at least 30 minutes.

Dust the work surface with flour. With a floured rolling pin, roll the dough into a small circle. Lift and rotate the dough and re-dust the surface lightly with flour as necessary. Continue to roll, rotate, and lift the dough until you form a 13-inch circle.

Drape the dough over the rolling pin and gently transfer the dough to a 9-inch pie pan, pressing it lightly into place. If necessary, trim the dough to a 1-inch overhang all around. Fold the dough over and crimp to form a thick, decorative edge.

For the bourbon pecan pie filling:
Preheat the oven to 375 degrees.

In a medium bowl, stir together the sugar and melted butter. Add the corn syrup, eggs, pecans, and bourbon. Stir until all ingredients are combined.

Pour the mixture into the unbaked pie shell and place on a heavy-duty cookie sheet. Bake for 10 minutes. Lower the oven temperature to 350 degrees and continue to bake until the pie is set, an additional 25 to 30 minutes.

Remove from the oven and cool on a wire rack.

Bread pudding

8 cups (½ gallon) milk

2 cups sugar

8 eggs, beaten

2 teaspoons vanilla extract

8 to 12 cups cubed white bread
    (about 18 slices)

1 cup golden raisins

1 tablespoon cinnamon

Maker's Mark bourbon sauce

½ cup (1 stick) butter

2 cups powdered sugar

¼ cup Maker's Mark bourbon

Makes 10 to 12 servings

Bread Pudding with Maker's Mark Bourbon Sauce

KEENELAND, LEXINGTON   ℒ   CHEF ED BOUTILIER

Located in the heart of Kentucky's Bluegrass region, Keeneland plays an important role in both Thoroughbred racing and breeding. During April and October race meets, a visit to Keeneland is sure to involve tailgating, bourbon-sipping, Kentucky-fine fashion, and an opportunity to enjoy this famous bread pudding and Keeneland Burgoo (see recipe in the Soups & Stews section, page 78).

For the bread pudding:
In a large bowl, whisk together the milk and sugar until the sugar dissolves. Add the eggs and vanilla and stir. Add the bread cubes and refrigerate for several hours or overnight to soak the bread with the mixture.

Preheat the oven to 275 degrees. Spray a 13 x 9 x 2-inch baking dish with nonstick spray.

Pour the bread cube mixture into the prepared baking pan. Sprinkle with the raisins and cinnamon and use a spoon to push the raisins into the mix. Bake until firm in the center and the liquid has cooked, about 1½ hours.

For the Maker's Mark bourbon sauce:
Allow the butter to soften at room temperature. Place in a mixing bowl and add the powdered sugar. Whip until well blended. Whip the bourbon into the mixture to a frosting consistency. Ladle the frosting over the hot bread pudding and it will melt on its own, making a sauce.

ℒ ***Note:*** *Allow time for the bread mixture to chill before baking. For a firmer pudding, use twelve cups of cubed bread instead of eight cups. Bake the bread pudding at a low temperature to fully cook the interior while leaving a soft crust.*

2 cups sugar

3 tablespoons flour

¾ cup buttermilk

4 eggs

4 tablespoons (½ stick) butter, melted

1 teaspoon vanilla extract

1 (9-inch) unbaked pie crust
(see butter pie crust recipe on page 127)

Makes 1 (9-inch) pie

Chess Pie

HAPPY HOUSE, MAYFIELD ❧ OWNER PAULINE RUSSELBURG

Known for serving one of the best lunches in Mayfield, the Happy House prepares food from scratch, including homemade desserts. Chess Pie is a popular pie in Kentucky and throughout the South. The name is somewhat of a mystery. Legend has it that it's either a variation of the phrase, "It's 'jes pie," or a variation of the name "chest pie," meaning a pie that stores well "in a chest" and without refrigeration because of its high sugar content. Some variations of Chess Pie add cornmeal to the filling, but Pauline uses 'jes flour.

Preheat the oven to 350 degrees.

In a bowl, stir together the sugar and flour. Whisk in the buttermilk until well blended. Beat in the eggs. Add the melted butter and vanilla, stirring well.

Pour the filling into the pie crust. Bake until the pie is cooked through, 55 to 60 minutes. Cool completely on a wire rack.

24 dried Mission figs

¾ cup Kentucky bourbon

24 roasted Marcona almonds
    or blanched almonds

1 (10-ounce) bag Ghirardelli 60%
    cacao bittersweet chocolate
    chips

Serves 8

Chocolate-Bourbon-Almond Stuffed Figs

ENOTECA, LEXINGTON
CHEF CARRIE ARPS

With one of the finest bourbon selections in Lexington, Enoteca's tapas menu includes these figs soaked in Willett's Johnny Drum bourbon. Sip a glass of tawny port to enhance the flavors as you sample the figs.

Place the figs in an airtight container and add the bourbon. Be sure that the figs have at least an inch of bourbon covering them, as they will soak up a lot of the bourbon. Soak the figs for 24 hours.

Drain the remaining bourbon from the figs. With a small paring knife, slit the bottom of each fig, making a hole to insert the almonds.

Stuff each fig with one roasted almond. (If you are using blanched almonds, spread them on a baking sheet and drizzle with extra virgin olive oil and salt. Preheat the oven to 350 degrees to roast the almonds. Bake until lightly browned.)

Place the chocolate in a double boiler and melt until smooth. Dip each fig into the chocolate, leaving the tip and stem exposed. Place the figs on parchment paper and refrigerate for at least 1 hour to harden the chocolate.

Bourbon praline topping

2 cups black walnuts or
    pecan halves

½ cup brown sugar

¼ cup heavy cream

2 tablespoons Kentucky bourbon

Tart crust

1 ½ cups flour

⅓ cup sugar

¼ teaspoon salt

½ cup (1 stick) cold butter, sliced

4 tablespoons cold water

Ganache

2 cups semi-sweet chocolate,
    chopped

1 ½ cups heavy cream

Makes 1 (9-inch) tart

Chocolate Tart with Bourbon Praline Topping

CLEMENTINE'S BAKE SHOP, BEREA
OWNERS LINDSEY WINDLAND AND DREW ELLIOTT

Clementine's boasts a menu of made-by-hand, from-scratch baked goods. Weisenberger Mill flour is a must, and black walnuts are classic, but if they aren't available, pecan halves are the perfect substitute.

For the bourbon praline topping:
Preheat the oven to 350 degrees.

In a medium bowl, combine the nuts, brown sugar, and cream. Spread onto a well-greased cookie sheet and bake for 20 minutes. Remove from the oven and allow to cool 5 minutes. Using a pastry brush, brush a few coats of bourbon onto the top of the pralines. Set aside to cool.

For the tart crust:
Spray one 9-inch tart pan with nonstick spray.

Combine the flour, sugar, salt, and butter in a food processor. Pulse for 20 seconds. The texture should be similar to coarse cornmeal. Pour into a large mixing bowl and sprinkle in the water, 1 tablespoon at a time, kneading after each addition. Stop when the dough forms a unified ball.

Press the dough into a large disk and sandwich between two pieces of parchment. With a rolling pin, flatten the disk and roll into a 12-inch circle to cover the bottom and sides of the tart pan. Remove the top layer of parchment. Flip the dough into the greased tart pan and carefully peel off the remaining parchment. Allow the dough to settle into the bottom and sides of the pan, gently pressing it into place. Fold any remaining dough into the pan and press it into the edges to form a thick border around the rim. Trim as necessary. Place the crust in the freezer to chill for 10 minutes.

Preheat the oven to 400 degrees. Remove the crust from the freezer, prick the bottom with a fork, and line the crust with aluminum foil, pressing to fit the shape of the dough. Fill the foil with dried beans (about 3 cups) or pie weights, spreading the beans or weights against the sides of the pan to prevent the crust from shrinking when it's baked. Fold the top of the foil over the beans away from the edge to expose the edge. Bake for 10 minutes. Reduce heat to 350 degrees and bake until golden brown, an additional 30 minutes. Remove the crust from the oven and carefully remove the bean-filled foil. Completely cool the crust on a wire rack.

For the ganache:
Place the chocolate in a heatproof bowl. In a saucepan, bring the cream to a simmer over medium-high heat. Pour the cream over the chocolate and allow to sit for 5 minutes. Whisk until smooth and then refrigerate to cool completely.

Once cool, beat with an electric mixer until double in size and light and fluffy. Spoon into the cooled crust, smooth the top with an offset spatula, and refrigerate. Before serving, sprinkle with the bourbon praline topping.

Pie crust

1 (9-inch) unbaked pie crust

Coconut filling

1 cup sugar

½ cup flour

¼ teaspoon salt

1 cup coconut flakes

3 cups milk

4 egg yolks

3 tablespoons butter

Meringue

4 egg whites

1 tablespoon sugar

¼ cup coconut flakes,
   lightly toasted if desired

Makes 1 (9-inch) pie

Coconut Cream Pie

GARRETT'S RESTAURANT, CARLISLE
GEORGE AND BECKY GARRETT

Famous for their pies and other homemade fare, this family-owned restaurant has been serving the city of Carlisle, and hungry travelers, for forty years. In this recipe, the coconut is cooked in the milk to infuse a coconut flavor throughout the custard, then the pie is topped with meringue and toasted coconut. For the pie dough, see butter pie crust recipe on page 127.

To prebake the pie crust:
Preheat the oven to 375 degrees. Roll out the pie dough and fit it into a 9-inch pie pan. Line the dough with foil and fill with dried beans or pie weights so the crust doesn't shrink. Fold the top of the foil over the beans away from the edge to expose the edge. Bake until the crust is browned and cooked, 25 to 30 minutes. Carefully remove the foil and beans. Cool the crust on a wire rack. Reduce the oven temperature to 350 degrees.

For the coconut filling:
While the pie shell is baking, in a saucepan over medium heat, combine the sugar, flour, salt, and 1 cup coconut flakes. Add the milk, bring to a boil, and cook until thickened.

In a separate bowl, whisk the eggs yolks. Slowly add some of the hot milk mixture to the egg yolks and whisk together. Stir the warmed egg yolks back into the saucepan and cook until the mixture is thick and a few large bubbles start to rise to the top. This will take a few minutes. Turn off the heat and stir in the butter to melt. Pour the filling into the prebaked pie shell.

For the meringue:
With an electric mixer, beat the egg whites on high speed. Add the sugar when the whites start to stiffen; continue beating until firm.

Spread the meringue evenly over the hot coconut pie filling and sprinkle with the ¼ cup coconut flakes. Bake at 350 degrees until slightly brown on top, 10 to 12 minutes. Let cool before slicing.

5 cups flour

3 tablespoons ground ginger

1 ½ tablespoons cinnamon

1 tablespoon plus 1 teaspoon
    baking soda

1 teaspoon salt

1 ½ cups (3 sticks) butter, softened

1 ¾ cups light brown sugar

½ cup molasses

2 eggs

2 tablespoons lemon zest

Makes 42 (3-inch) cookies

Ginger Gems

THE MIDWAY BAKERY, MIDWAY   &   CHEF CARRIE WARMBIER

Housed in an old school building, The Midway Bakery bakes everything by hand, using real ingredients. Their flour, chocolate, and nuts are sourced from Kentucky. These cookies are a nod to the historical significance of gingerbread in Kentucky's political history, when candidates handed out gingerbread cakes on Election Day to win votes. Ginger Gems freeze well and are perfect for boxed cookie gifts.

Preheat the oven to 350 degrees. Line baking sheets with parchment paper.

In a large bowl, whisk together the flour, ground ginger, cinnamon, baking soda, and salt.

In a separate bowl, cream the butter and sugar until light and fluffy. Add the molasses and blend well. Add the eggs and lemon zest and mix well, then add the dry ingredients and mix until well incorporated.

Use a cookie scoop to portion out balls of dough. Roll the dough into balls and place on the parchment-lined baking sheet. Leave plenty of space so the cookies can spread, about eight cookies per sheet. Flatten slightly with a floured hand.

Bake, rotating the sheet midway, until very lightly browned around the edges, 12 to 14 minutes. Cool on the pan until the cookies begin to firm up, and then transfer to wire cooling racks.

Harvest Rum Balls

WILDERNESS TRAIL DISTILLERY, DANVILLE
OWNER JEROD SMITH

A craft distillery, Wilderness Trail is the oldest legal distillery in Danville. They produce unique rum handmade from locally grown Kentucky sweet sorghum molasses and aged in used Kentucky bourbon barrels. Also known as "the Bourbon Drinkers Rum," Harvest Rum presents a bourbon front and sweet rum finish. Danny Townsend, of Townsend Sorghum Mill, an expert on sorghum molasses, selects the batches that turn into Harvest Rum. This recipe is a twist on a favorite Kentucky candy—bourbon balls—using Harvest Rum in place of bourbon.

1 pound powdered sugar

⅓ cup Wilderness Trail Harvest Rum

4 tablespoons (½ stick) butter, softened

½ cup finely chopped pecans

1 (10-ounce) bag Ghirardelli 60% cacao bittersweet chocolate chips

36 pecan halves, for garnish

Makes 36 rum balls

With an electric mixer, blend the sugar, rum, butter, and pecans until a soft dough forms. Refrigerate for at least 8 hours or overnight.

Melt the chocolate over a double boiler. Using a small scoop, portion out the dough. Roll into 1-inch balls and dip in the melted chocolate. Garnish with pecan halves. Refrigerate to harden the chocolate.

❧ ***Note:*** *To make bourbon balls, substitute Kentucky bourbon for the rum and proceed with the recipe as directed.*

1 sheet frozen puff pastry

¼ cup Bird Dog Cinnamon Whiskey

1 cup dried cherries

3 local apples, cored, halved, and sliced thinly

½ cup Kentucky chestnuts

4 tablespoons (½ stick) butter, cut into pieces

½ cup brown sugar

2 tablespoons apple cider vinegar

1 ½ teaspoons cinnamon

2 tablespoons butter, melted

1 teaspoon cinnamon (for dusting)

3 tablespoons smoked sugar or other coarse sugar

¼ cup local honey

2 tablespoons powdered sugar

Serves 8

Jackson's Orchard Apple Strudel

HOME CAFÉ & MARKETPLACE, BOWLING GREEN
EXECUTIVE CHEF AND OWNER JOSHUA POLING

Chef Poling's strudel features local apples from Jackson's Orchard, Kentucky chestnuts, cinnamon whiskey, and Bourbon Barrel Foods Smoked Sugar. The result is a unique combination of flavors and textures wrapped in a sweet, flaky crust.

Thaw puff pastry on the countertop for 40 minutes.

Preheat the oven to 375 degrees. Line a baking sheet with parchment paper.

In a small bowl, pour the whiskey over the cherries and microwave on high for 45 seconds. Let sit for 15 minutes.

In a large bowl, combine the cherries, apples, chestnuts, butter pieces, brown sugar, vinegar, and cinnamon.

Lightly dust a work surface with flour. Lay the puff pastry on top and dust the rolling pin with additional flour. Gently roll the puff pastry to ⅛-inch thickness.

Spread the apple mixture over the bottom half of the puff pastry square, leaving about 1 inch of space along the side edges. Fold the top half of the puff pastry over and pinch to seal the edges together.

Brush the entire strudel with the melted butter and then sprinkle with cinnamon and smoked sugar. Using a serrated knife, make three diagonal slits across the top of the strudel.

Place the strudel on the parchment-lined baking sheet and bake, rotating the sheet halfway through baking, until the pastry is puffed and golden brown, about 40 minutes.

When slightly cooled, drizzle with honey and dust with powdered sugar. Serve warm.

Shortbread crust

2 cups flour

½ cup powdered sugar

¾ cup (1 ½ sticks) cold butter,
    cut in small pieces

Zest of half a lemon

Lemon filling

4 eggs

1 ½ cups sugar

⅓ cup flour

1 teaspoon baking powder

¼ cup lemon juice (2 to 3 lemons)

Zest of half a lemon

Lemon glaze

1 cup powdered sugar

1 ½ tablespoons fresh lemon juice

Serves 12

Lemon Bars

THE MIDWAY BAKERY, MIDWAY   ❧   CHEF CARRIE WARMBIER

*Everything baked at The Midway Bakery is made with real ingredients—
no fillers, gels, or stabilizers—just butter, sugar, cream, and chocolate.
Lemons aren't native to Kentucky, but they are the star of many popular
Kentucky desserts. These lemon bars have a thick crust and are topped
with a lemon glaze instead of the traditional powdered sugar.*

For the shortbread crust:
Preheat the oven to 350 degrees.

Mix the flour and ½ cup powdered sugar in a large bowl. Cut the
butter into the flour and sugar mixture until it becomes crumbly. Add
the lemon zest and mix well until the dough holds together. Divide
evenly in a 10 x 7-inch baking pan and press into a level crust.

Bake the crust until lightly browned around the edges, 12 to 15
minutes. Cool on a wire rack to room temperature while mixing
the filling.

For the lemon filling:
In a large bowl, mix together the eggs, sugar, flour, baking powder,
lemon juice, and lemon zest. Pour evenly over the baked and cooled
crust. Bake until the custard is set, 25 to 30 minutes. Let cool.

For the lemon glaze:
Mix the 1 cup powdered sugar and lemon juice. Spoon the glaze
over the filling and spread evenly with a knife. Be careful to not pull
up the top of the filling while glazing. When the glaze is set, cut into
bars with a knife.

(see photograph on page 123)

Marbled pound cake

3 cups cake flour, sifted

1 teaspoon baking powder

½ teaspoon baking soda

1 teaspoon salt

1 cup (2 sticks) butter,
    at room temperature

1½ cups granulated sugar

½ cup light brown sugar,
    packed firm

4 eggs

1 cup buttermilk

¼ cup Kentucky bourbon

3 tablespoons cocoa powder

Bourbon glaze

6 tablespoons butter

¾ cup sugar

¼ cup Kentucky bourbon

Makes 1 (10-inch) tube cake

Marbled Bourbon Pound Cake

THE GREEN APRON COMPANY, FT. WRIGHT   ❧   MAGGIE GREEN

Pound cakes are a tradition in the South. When soaked with a bourbon-spiked glaze, this chocolate-marbled variation makes a Kentucky-style dessert that slices beautifully and stores well for several days.

For the marbled pound cake:
Preheat the oven to 350 degrees. Thoroughly spray a 10-inch tube pan with nonstick baking spray and dust with flour. Alternatively, grease and flour the pan.

In a medium bowl, sift together the cake flour, baking powder, baking soda, and salt.

In the bowl of a stand mixer, cream together the butter, granulated sugar, and brown sugar on medium speed until light and fluffy, about 5 minutes. Turn the mixer to low and add the eggs one at a time. Scrape the bowl to be sure all the butter, sugar, and eggs are well blended.

In a small bowl, whisk together the buttermilk and bourbon.

Add the flour mixture to the butter and eggs in three parts, alternating with the buttermilk and beginning and ending with the flour. After each addition, scrape the bowl.

Using a 2-cup measuring cup, remove 1 cup of batter from the bowl. Stir the cocoa powder into this cup of batter.

Pour half of the remaining plain batter into the prepared pan. Top with three or four large spoonfuls of the chocolate batter. Add the rest of the plain batter and finish with any remaining chocolate batter. Gently tap the pan on the countertop. With a thin knife, swirl the batter together several times in a zigzag motion to spread the chocolate batter throughout the cake batter. Don't overdo it.

Bake until the cake is lightly browned on the edges and springs back in the center when lightly pressed with a finger, 55 to 60 minutes. Remove from the oven and let rest on a cooling rack while you prepare the glaze.

For the bourbon glaze:
In a saucepan, whisk together the butter, sugar, and bourbon over low heat just until the butter melts and the sugar dissolves. Do not allow the mixture to boil or it will become hard.

To glaze the cake:
With a long, thin skewer, poke holes all over the exposed top of the cake. Drizzle half of the glaze on the cake, allowing the glaze to soak into the holes and into the cake. Let cool for 30 minutes.

Turn the cake out onto a platter so the glazed side is down. Reheat the glaze if necessary to thin and drizzle or brush over the top of the cake.

7 egg whites

1½ cups sugar

1½ cups graham cracker crumbs

1½ cups chopped pecans

1½ cups flaked coconut

1 (9-inch) unbaked pie crust

2 medium bananas, sliced

2 cups sweetened whipped cream

Makes 1 (9-inch) pie

Patti's Sawdust Pie

PATTI'S 1880'S SETTLEMENT, GRAND RIVERS
GENERAL MANAGER ANITA WILLIAMSON

Opened in 1977 as Hamburger Patti's Ice Cream Parlor, this restaurant is an institution in the Land Between The Lakes National Recreation Area in western Kentucky. Patti's signature pie was named Sawdust Pie because some say it looks like baked sawdust. For a pie crust recipe, see the Bourbon Pecan Pie recipe in Desserts & Sweet Treats, page 127.

Preheat the oven to 350 degrees.

In a large bowl, stir the egg whites, sugar, graham cracker crumbs, pecans, and coconut until well blended. Pour into the unbaked pie shell.

Bake until the filling is glossy and set, 35 to 40 minutes. Do not over-bake! When done, the center should be gooey.

Serve warm topped with sliced bananas and whipped cream.

Batter

½ cup (1 stick) butter

1 cup flour

1 cup sugar

1 teaspoon baking powder

1 cup milk

Filling

2 cups fresh peach slices
    or blackberries

¾ cup sugar

2 tablespoons flour

Serves 8

Peach Cobbler

BOYCE GENERAL STORE, ALVATON   ❧   BRIE AND BRAD GOLLIHER

This "deconstructed" cobbler is simple to make but every bit as delicious as its fancier counterparts. Substitute fresh blackberries, Kentucky's favorite summertime fruit, for the peaches if desired, or you can even use half peaches and half blackberries for a mixed-fruit cobbler.

For the batter:
Preheat the oven to 350 degrees.

Place the butter in an 8 x 8 x 2-inch glass baking dish and put it in the oven to melt, about 10 minutes. Meanwhile, in a bowl combine the flour, sugar, baking powder, and milk.

For the filling:
In another bowl, combine the fruit, ¾ cup sugar, and 2 tablespoons flour.

To assemble:
When the butter is melted, remove the baking dish from the oven and pour the batter over the melted butter. Do not stir. Then place spoonfuls of fruit on top of the batter. Again, do not stir.

Bake until bubbly and brown, 50 to 60 minutes. Serve warm with a scoop of vanilla bean ice cream.

sources for specialty ingredients and other products

Alltech Brewing and Distilling Company: online at kentuckyale.com

Beer Cheese Trail: online at beercheesetrail.com

Bird Dog Cinnamon Whiskey: online at birddogwhiskey.com

Bison at KY Bison Co.: online at woodlandfarm.com

Black walnuts: online at black-walnuts.com

Bleugrass Chevre Farmstead Goat Cheese: online at bleugrasschevre.com

Boone Creek Creamery: online at boonecreekcreamery.com

Bourbon Barrel Foods Worcestershire sauce, smoked paprika, soy sauce, smoked salt, sorghum, and smoked sugar: sold nationwide and online at bourbonbarrelfoods.com

Boursin Cheese: most major supermarkets and online at boursin.com

Bragg Nutritional Yeast Seasoning: natural food section of supermarkets or online at bragg.com

Brewgrass Trail: online at brewgrasstrail.com

Broadbent's Kentucky Country Ham, Bacon, and Sausage: online at broadbenthams.com

Brookview Farm Kentucky grass-fed, grass-finished beef: in Winchester or online at brookviewbeef.com

Bulleit Bourbon: online at bulleitbourbon.com

Capriole Goat Cheese: online at capriolegoatcheese.com

Col. Bill Newsom's Aged Kentucky Country Ham: online at newsomscountryham.com

Colibri Sheep Farm: online at colibrisheep.com

Colonel De Gourmet Herbs & Spices: Jungle Jim's, Friendly Market, Historic Findlay Market, and online at colonelde.com

Country Boy Brewing: online at countryboybrewing.com

Crystal Hot Sauce: Kroger, Remke Market, Kremer's Market, and online at baumerfoods.com

Downing Cattle Company, Inc. all natural beef and pork: online at downingcattlecompanyinc.com

Duke's Mayonnaise: most major supermarkets in the South and online at dukesmayo.com

Early Times Kentucky Whisky: online at earlytimes.com

Father's Country Hams: online at fatherscountryhams.com

Fig Balsamic Vinegar and Olive Oil: Stuarto's in Lexington or online at stuartos.com

Food Chain Urban Farm: online at foodchainlex.org

Four Hills Farm: Good Foods Co-Op in Lexington

Four Petal Farm: online at fourpetalfarm.com

George Gagel Truck Farm's Limestone Bibb Lettuce: Gagel Farm Market and online at gagels.com

Ghirardelli Chocolate: most supermarkets and online at ghirardelli.com

Greensleeves Farm: online at greensleevesfarm.wordpress.com

Grippo's Potato Chips: most supermarkets and online at grippos.com

Groganica Aquaponic Farm: online at facebook.com/groganica

Harper's Country Ham: online at hamtastic.com

Harvest Rum: Kroger, Liquor Barn, and online at wildernesstraildistillery.com

HF Farms CSA and fresh produce: online at hffarms.net

Hickoryworks Syrup: online at hickoryworks.homestead.com

Hood's Heritage Hogs featuring Red Wattle Pork: Lexington Farmers Market or online at hoodsheritagehogs.com

Jackson's Orchard Apples: online at jacksonsorchard.com

Kenny's Cheese for cheese curds and other farmhouse cheese: Jungle Jim's, Kremer's Market, Party Source, and online at kennyscheese.com

Kentucky Bourbon Barrel Ale: most liquor stores or kentuckyale.com

Kentucky Bourbon Trail: online at kybourbontrail.com

Kentucky Colonel Mint: online at wilsonnurseriesky.com

Kentucky Kernel Seasoned Flour: most major supermarkets and online at hodgsonmillstore.com

Kentucky Maple Syrup: online at federalgrove.com

Kentucky Proud, Kentucky's marketing brand and program for KY Agriculture and the commonwealth's local foods: online at kyproud.com

Kentucky Wonder Pole Beans: save seeds or online at seedsaver.org

Leaf Lard, along with eggs, beef, and pork: online at ashbournefarms.com

Maddie's Gold Smoked Cheese: Ed-Mar Dairy, Brooks Meats, Friendly Meats, Kremer's Market, and online at ed-mardairy.com

Maker's Mark Bourbon: online at makersmark.com

Marcona almonds: Trader Joe's, Costco, or online at nuts.com

Marksbury Farm Market beef, sausage, and pork: Whole Foods Market, Good Foods Co-op, and online at marksburyfarm.com

Moonlite Bar-B-Q Sauce: online at moonlite.com

Natural Hog Casings: Jungle Jim's or online at qualitycasing.com

Need More Acres Farm CSA: online at needmoreacres.com

Old Bay Seasoning: most major supermarkets and online at oldbay.com

Old Hickory Hill hickory syrup: online at oldhickoryhill.com

Ramps: found through foraging, sometimes at farmers markets, or online at kingofstink.com

Reed Valley Orchard apples and berries: online at reedvalleyorchard.com

Shiitake mushrooms from Sheltowee Farm Gourmet Mushrooms: Lexington Farmers Market and online at sheltoweefarm.com

Stone Cross Farm Kentucky beef and pork: online at stonecrossfarm.com

Tamari Wheat-Free Soy Sauce: Asian cooking section of supermarkets or online at san-j.com

Townsend Sorghum Mill sorghum syrup (featured in Wilderness Trail's Harvest Rum): online at townsendsorghummill.com

Weisenberger Mill flour, cornmeal, and grits: local Kroger stores, Friendly Market, and online at weisenberger.com

West Sixth Brewery Ales and Lagers: Kroger, Liquor Barn, and online at westsixth.com

Wild Kentucky Pecans from Kentucky Nut Corporation: online at kykernelpecans.com

Willett's Johnny Drum Bourbon: online at kentuckybourbonwhiskey.com

Wind Stone Farms Blackberry Jam: Kroger, Remke, or Kremer's Market or online at windstonefarms.com

Woodford Reserve Kentucky Straight Bourbon: online at woodfordreserve.com

contributors

610 Magnolia
610 Magnolia Avenue
Louisville, KY 40208
(502) 636-0783
elee@aol.com
610magnolia.com

Against the Grain Brewery and Smokehouse
401 East Main Street
Louisville, KY 40202
(502) 515-0174
jordan@atgbrewery.com
atgbrewery.com

Aurora Landing
Ken Lake State Resort Park
542 Kenlake Road
Hardin, KY 42048
(270) 474-2211
thomas.brown@ky.gov
parks.ky.gov

AZUR Restaurant & Patio
Beaumont Centre
3070 Lakecrest Circle, Suite 550
Lexington, KY 40513
(859) 296-1007
chefjashby@gmail.com
azurrestaurant.com

The Blue Raven Restaurant & Pub
211 Main Street
Pikeville, KY 41501
(859) 608-8101
matt_corbin2@me.com
theblueraven.net

Bluebird
202 West Main Street
Stanford, KY 40484
(606) 365-1010
stanford.bluebird@gmail.com
bluebirdnatural.com

Bourbon Manor Bed & Breakfast
714 North 3rd Street
Bardstown, KY 40004
(502) 350-1010
stay@bourbonmanor.com
bourbonmanor.com

Boyce General Store
10551 Woodburn Allen Springs Road
Alvaton, KY 42122
(270) 842-1900
boycegeneralstore@gmail.com
facebook.com/boycegeneralstore

Brasabana Cuban Cuisine
841 Lane Allen Road
Lexington, KY 40504
(859) 303-5573
chefjashby@gmail.com
brasabana.com

The Brown Hotel
335 West Broadway
Louisville, KY 40202
(502) 583-1234
Jbettis@brownhotel.com
brownhotel.com

Cadiz Restaurant
324 Main Street
Cadiz, KY 42211
(270) 522-2249

Clementine's Bake Shop
3337 Scaffold Cane Road
Berea, KY 40403
(859) 756-3031
clementinesbakery@gmail.com
facebook.com/clementinesbakeshop

Cue on Main
303 West Main Street
Danville, KY 40422
(859) 236-2400
wallybremer2@yahoo.com
cueonmain-hub.com

Distilled at Gratz Park Inn
120 West 2nd Street
Lexington, KY 40507
(859) 255-0002
distilledatgratzpark@gmail.com
distilledatgratzparkinn.com

Ed-Mar Dairy
1034 Walton-Nicholson Road
Walton, KY 41051
(859) 620-1860
info@ed-mardairy.com
ed-mardairy.com

Enoteca
191 Jefferson Street
Lexington, KY 40502
(859) 687-0346
enotecalex@gmail.com
enotecalex.com

Equus & Jack's Lounge
122 Sears Avenue
Louisville, KY 40207
(502) 897-9721
arnett.equus@gmail.com
equusrestaurant.com

Fork in the Road Mobile Galley
Anywhere Street
Lexington, KY 40502
(859) 309-9854
info@middleforkkb.com
middleforkkb.com

Garrett's Restaurant
215 North Broadway
Carlisle, KY 40311
(859) 289-7582
georgegarrett@bellsouth.net
facebook.com/garretts-restaurant

Glenn's Creek Café
7855 McCracken Pike
Versailles, KY 40383
(859) 879-1921
pchieb33@gmail.com
woodfordreserve.com

Gold Rush Cafe
400 Broadway Street
Paducah, KY 42001
(270) 443-4422

Graze Market and Cafe
150 Combs Ferry
Winchester, KY 40391
(859) 745-0990
cadevilliers@gmail.com
grazelex.com

The Green Apron Company
2335 Buttermilk Crossing, Suite 341
Crescent Spring, KY 41011
(859) 344-8403
maggie@greenapron.com
greenapron.com

Greyhound Tavern
2500 Dixie Highway
Ft. Mitchell, KY 41017
(859) 331-3767
greyhoundtavern@fuse.net
greyhoundtavern.com

Happy House Restaurant
236 North 8th Street
Mayfield, KY 42066
(270) 247-5743

Harrison-Smith House
103 East Stephen Foster Avenue
Bardstown, KY 40004
(502) 233-9993
info@harrisonsmithhouse.com
harrisonsmithhouse.com

Heirloom
125 East Main
Midway, KY 40347
(859) 846-5565
markwombles@gmail.com
heirloommidway.com

Holly Hill Inn
426 North Winter Street
Midway, KY 40347
(859) 846-4732
hollyhillmidway@aol.com
hollyhillinn.com

Home Café & Marketplace
2440 Nashville Road, Suite 108
Bowling Green, KY 42101
(270) 846-1272
info@homecafebg.com
homecafebg.com

Island View Restaurant
Dale Hollow Lake State Resort Park
5970 State Park Road
Burkesville, KY 42717
(270) 433-7431
thomas.brown@ky.gov
parks.ky.gov

Keeneland
4201 Versailles Road
Lexington, KY 40504
(800) 456-3412
info@keeneland.com
keeneland.com

Kentucky Proud Kitchen
136 Towne Square Park
Lexington, KY 40511
brigittecooks@gmail.com
brigittecooks.com

Maple Hill Manor Bed & Breakfast
2941 Perryville Road
Springfield, KY 40069
(859) 481-4403
stay@maplehillmanor.com
maplehillmanor.com

Marksbury Farm Market
7907 Nicholasville Road
Lancaster, KY 40444
(859) 754-4224
wsarbacker@marksburyfarm.com
marksburyfarm.com

middle fork kitchen bar
1224 Manchester Street
Lexington, KY 40502
(859) 309-9854
info@middleforkkb.com
middleforkkb.com

The Midway Bakery
510 South Winter Street
Midway, KY 40347
(859) 846-4336
info@midwayschoolbakery.com
midwayschoolbakery.com

Milkwood
316 West Main Street
Louisville, KY 40202
(502) 584-6455
elee@aol.com
milkwoodrestaurant.com

The Miller House
301 East 5th Street
Owensboro, KY 42301
(270) 685-5878
kaseykirk@gmail.com
themillerhouserestaurant.com

Moonlite Bar-B-Q Inn
2840 West Parrish Avenue
Owensboro, KY 42303
(270) 684-8143
email@moonlite.com
moonlite.com

Need More Acres Farm
395 Hickory Lane
Scottsville, KY 42164
(270) 799-5563
michelle.lifeisgood@gmail.com
needmoreacres.com

Otto's
521 Main Street
Covington, KY 41011
(859) 491-6678
paulweckman@yahoo.com
ottosonmain.com

Patti's 1880's Settlement
1793 J. H. O'Bryan Avenue
Grand Rivers, KY 42045
(270) 362-8844
anita@pattis-settlement.com
pattis-settlement.com

Pop's Southern Style BBQ
110 KY Highway 801 South
Morehead, KY 40351
(606) 784-6378
popsssbbq@yahoo.com
facebook.com/popsssbbq

Red River Rockhouse
4000 Route 11
Campton, KY 41301
(606) 668-6656
tina@redriverrockhouse.com
redriverrockhouse.com

Smithtown Seafood
501 West 6th Street
Lexington, KY 40508
(859) 303-4100
info@smithtownseafood.com
smithtownseafood.com

Snug Hollow Farm Bed & Breakfast
790 McSwain Branch
Irvine, KY 40336
(606) 723-4786
info@snughollow.com
snughollow.com

Spoonful of Sugar . . .
Sweets and Such
18 West Main Street
Mt. Sterling, KY 40353
(859) 497-1955
petite127@bellsouth.net
spoonfulofsugarsweetsandsuch.com

The Tousey House Tavern
5963 Jefferson Street
Burlington, KY 41051
(859) 586-9900
touseyhouse@fuse.net
touseyhouse.com

The Trustees' Table at Shaker Village
of Pleasant Hill
3501 Lexington Road
Harrodsburg, KY 40330
(859) 734-5411
info@shakervillageky.org
shakervillageky.org

The Village Anchor
11507 Park Road
Anchorage, KY 40223
(502) 708-1850
goeff@villageanchor.com
villageanchor.com

Wallace Station Deli
3854 Old Frankfort Pike
Versailles, KY
(859) 846-5161
genie@wallacestation.com
wallacestation.com

Wilderness Trail Distillery
445 Roy Arnold Avenue
Danville, KY 40422
(859) 402-8707
jerod.smith@wildernesstrailky.com
wildernesstraildistillery.com

Wiltshire On Market
636 East Market Street
Louisville, KY 40202
(502) 589-5224
jonathonexum@gmail.com
wiltshirepantry.com/wiltshire-
on-market

Wiltshire Pantry
1310 East Breckenridge Street
Louisville, KY 40204
(502) 581-8560
wiltshirepantry@gmail.com
wiltshirepantry.com

Windy Corner Market
4595 Bryan Stations Road
Lexington, KY 40516
(859) 294-9338
genie@windycornermarket.com
windycornermarket.com

Winston's
3101 Bardstown Road
Louisville, KY 40204
(502) 456-0980
agscott@sullivan.edu
winstonsoflouisville.com

Woodford Reserve Distillery
7855 McCracken Pike
Versailles, KY 40383
(859) 879-1921
woodfordreserve.com/distillery/
distillery-events

Wunderbar Covington
1132 Lee Street
Covington, KY 41011
(859) 815-8027
wunderbarcovington@gmail.com
wunderbarcovington.com

index